Unto the Daughters

The Legacy of an

Honor Killing

in a Sicilian-American Family

Karen Tintori

St. Martin's Griffin ♞ New York

www.stmartins.com

Design by Kathryn Parise

Library of Congress Cataloging-in-Publication Data

Tintori, Karen.
    Unto the daughters : the legacy of an honor killing in a Sicilian-American family / Karen Tintori.
        p. cm.
    ISBN-13: 978-0-312-33464-2
    ISBN-10: 0-312-33464-8
    1. Costa, Francesca—Death and burial. 2. Honor killings—Michigan—Detroit. 3. Victims of family violence—Michigan—Detroit. 4. Italian Americans—Michigan—Detroit—social life and customs—20th century. I. Title.

HV6197.D4 T56 2007
364.152'3092—dc22

                                                                2007012922

First St. Martin's Griffin Edition: July 2008

P 1

For
Grace
Joanne
and, always,
Frances

Nowhere has truth so short a life as in Sicily; a fact has scarcely happened five minutes before its genuine kernel has vanished, been camouflaged, embellished, disfigured, squashed, annihilated by imagination and self-interest; shame, fear, generosity, malice, opportunism, charity, all the passions, good as well as evil, fling themselves onto the fact and tear it to pieces; very soon it has vanished altogether.

    —GIUSEPPE DI LAMPEDUSA, *The Leopard*

To DETROIT

In the street you see nothing but people begging, day by day, and what's more revolting still is that there are people begging for just enough money to buy themselves a piece of bread. Cursed country! In Sicily, they're born like beasts and they die like beasts—but you go to America as a beast and you become a man!

    —GAVIN MAXWELL, *The Ten Pains of Death*

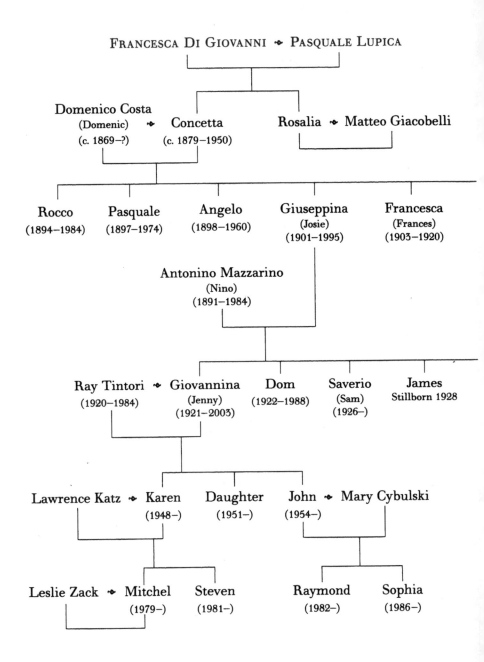

Praise for *Unto the Daughters*

"Many books are called 'page-turners' by reviewers, but this one will truly have you glued to the turning pages for hours. It's a must-read for anyone researching their Italian ancestry."
—*Comunes of Italy* magazine

"Nearly every family has a skeleton in its closet, an ancestor who 'sins' against custom and tradition and pays a double price— ostracism or worse at the time, and obliteration from the memory of succeeding generations. Few of these transgressors paid a higher price than Frances Costa, who was brutally murdered by her own brothers in a 1919 Sicilian honor killing in Detroit. And fewer yet have had a more tenacious successor than Frances's great-niece, Karen Tintori, who refused to allow the truth to remain forgotten. This is a book for anyone who shares the conviction that all history, in the end, is family history."
—Frank Viviano, author of *Blood Washes Blood* and
Dispatches from the Pacific Century

"Tintori's poignant memoir of the recent discovery of her great-aunt's murder deeply underscores her Sicilian culture's troubling subjugation of its women." —*Publishers Weekly*

"Switching back and forth between rural Sicily and early twentieth-century Detroit, *Unto the Daughters* reads like a nonfiction version of the film *The Godfather: Part II*—if it had been told from the point of view of a female Corleone. In exploring her own family's secret history, Karen Tintori gives voice not just to her victimized aunt but to all Italian-American daughters and wives silenced by the power of *omerta*. Half gripping true-crime story, half moving family memoir, *Unto the Daughters* is both fascinating and frightening, packed with telling details and obscure folklore that help bring the suffocating world of a Mafia family to life."
—Eleni N. Gage, author of *North of Ithaka*

Unto
the
Daughters

Also by Karen Tintori

Trapped: The 1909 Cherry Mine Disaster

The Book of Names (with Jill Gregory)

The Illuminator (with Jill Gregory)

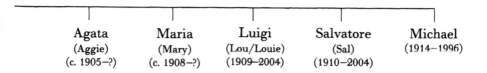

Agata	Maria	Luigi	Salvatore	Michael
(Aggie)	(Mary)	(Lou/Louie)	(Sal)	(1914–1996)
(c. 1905–?)	(c. 1908–?)	(1909–2004)	(1910–2004)	

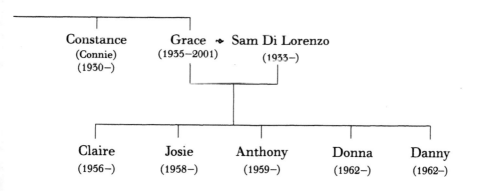

Constance	Grace ⚭ Sam Di Lorenzo	
(Connie)	(1935–2001)	(1933–)
(1930–)		

Claire	Josie	Anthony	Donna	Danny
(1956–)	(1958–)	(1959–)	(1962–)	(1962–)

Unto
the
Daughters

Prologue ❖

Four generations—my mother, me on Great-Grandma Concetta's lap, Josie Mazzarino.

Captured together only once, in a black-and-white photo, we are four females squinting into the future from a back porch in Detroit. Sunlight glows across my mother's light floral print dress. A smile lights her dark, pretty face as she leans easily toward her grandmother and her firstborn, exuding confidence in her new role as my mom. My Gramma Josie flanks Great-Grandma Concetta from the opposite side. She stands stout, stiff, and proud, one hand resting along her mother's back while the other holds my cloth drool diaper.

I can almost hear the glee in my clapping baby hands as they respond to the photographer. I sit, eager and one year old, in the lap of my frowning great-grandmother, years away from the conviction that I never want a daughter of my own.

I am the eldest daughter of the eldest daughter of the eldest daughter in a chain of daughters only two generations removed from the soil of Sicily.

When I was thirteen, my parents hammered home that I was going to college, I wasn't getting married until I completed my education, and I wasn't moving out of the house until I was married.

When my mother was fourteen, her mother took to her bed for a year and her parents made her drop out of school to wash, iron, cook, clean, and tend to their family of seven, which included a newborn.

When my grandmother was fifteen, and engaged to my grandfather, her father beat her purple and locked her in her room because she had handed her fiancé his hat.

When Frances, her younger sister, was sixteen, the unspeakable happened.

Detroit, July 13, 1961

I am drowning. I am thirteen and I cannot swim.

Everything is gray and quiet. Suspended, and still. I am stunned by that, thinking—

So this is death.

Infinitely less violent than I would have guessed. Nothing at all like the boiled-in-oil, raped-to-death, skinned-alive martyrs' demises the nuns had recounted to us, christening each school day with another grisly tale from the worn, ribbon-marked pages of their blood-red storybook, *Lives of the Saints.* One martyred role model for each day. Spoon-fed sacred sustenance for our young

Catholic souls, sandwiched between Mass and math and digested with the cold buttered toast wrapped in waxed paper and the warm white milk I bring from home to break my Communion fast.

I am amazed to be so aware, so accepting, so relaxed, enveloped there in that soothing silence. Airless. Peaceful. Motionless. Gray. It's as if I'm peering at infinity through opaque eyelids.

Calmly, curiously, I turn these observations over in my mind, examining them like the whorls of some exotic seashell, yet on another level I know that only a minute ago I was churning up the water like a wounded octopus, fighting desperately to plant my feet again on the lake's shifting bottom, grabbing for the rope marking off this private beach, or for my sister, Margaret, who stands hollering next to me, struggling against the waves eddying from behind the motorboat that knocked me off balance in chest-deep water as it angled away from the opposite shoreline with a cargo of giddy campers. Each time I gargle to the surface for help, wishing to God my father hadn't ducked into the woods to change into his bathing suit, counting off mentally—one, then two, then three—each time my head goes under.

I am struck by how immensely calm it is here—at death. Why should I have ever been afraid to die? This is so easy. I'd read once that drowning was excruciating—that your lungs burst like overblown balloons, flooding your guts with the water you'd sucked down in a last frantic gasp at life. I'd envisioned being terrified, coughing and sputtering, arms and legs flailing in a desperate panic to break the surface, to right myself, get my feet back on the sandy bottom. I should be screaming to my father's cousin Fred, who invited us here: "HELP ME! I DON'T KNOW HOW TO SWIM!"

Instead, I linger in this pearly limbo—waiting, wading—as my milky surroundings segue into a hazy tunnel hung with filmy lengths of plastic dry cleaners' bags. I know this place. . . .

. . .

As I crawl down the familiar varnished floor of Gramma Mazzarino's narrow upstairs closet, I send dust bunnies scuttling. The closet trails along the outside wall of the house, a tunnel connecting the front and back bedrooms, a secret hiding place the girl cousins discovered while our mothers lingered in the dining room over the last of the cannolis and sugared coffee, visiting and one-upping each other with their kids' scholastic accomplishments until they could delay no longer scrubbing out the sinkful of soaking pots. They chattered in the Sicilian dialect of our grandparents' villages when they didn't want us to understand, but somehow, with the help of the few English words they threw in, we always understood when they were talking about us.

The closet was our place to hide and share our own secrets while our fathers downed their frosty Pabst Blue Ribbons and shouted at the Philco TV's fuzzy black-and-white football game or at each other, bellowing out numbers—*due, quattro, cinque*—while they flung out their fingers in a raucous game that reminds me of paper, scissors, rock. But this game is called *morra*, the Sicilian word for *morta*—"death."

Faint daylight shimmers down through the closet's single window, Priscilla-curtained and overlooking Grandpa Mazzarino's back garden. Below, his prized apricot tree sways, its golden nuggets just out of my reach. Beyond the door ahead of me, in the bedroom's shadows, an ominous walnut dresser lurks in the corner beneath its carved oval mirror. I like to imagine it as the one in which my great-grandmother stored the Quincy apples my grandmother coveted when she was a little girl. When I imagine her mother walking into the room, I close my mind.

"Oh my God. Oh my God!"

My father's voice floats out of the woods like a sail billowing toward me on his breath. "For Chrissakes, GET HER!"

Then Daddy is running out of the woods and past my mother,

down the short, grass-splotched beach, crashing into the water, his T-shirt white as a beam from a lighthouse.

Four rude hands hoist me, shattering my solitary gray reverie. My father and Fred drag me sputtering over silt and thready weeds. Sand and tiny pebbles grit between my toes as they run toward the picnic tables, stubbing my feet against the uneven carpet of beach. Coughing and choking, I crumple to the wet sand, and nothing is peaceful any longer.

Air sears my nasal passages and throat but I can't suck down enough of it and I'm choking and sobbing and gasping and puking into a foamy puddle spreading between my mother's knees.

"Fred thought you girls were just goofing around out there," my mother says. "He didn't know you can't swim."

I swipe back the strands of hair dripping in my eyes and turn toward my father's voice. Calm. Reassuring. Insisting I'll be just fine. Blinking away the lake water and my tears, I'm shocked to see that my father isn't wearing a white T-shirt at all. My lighthouse is actually Daddy's bare milky chest framed by his sun-bronzed face and forearms.

Against my mother's protests, within the hour he has me back in that lake, insisting for probably the hundredth time in my life that he is going to prove to me that I can swim. He'd taken a rare day off from work that Friday for our family picnic on the private beach opposite a church's summer camp, and he was not about to take me home more frightened of the water than I was before.

"Relax. Just float," he coaches, same as he always does, whooping encouragement as I bob facedown with my midriff teetering on the fulcrum of his outstretched forearms. But it's no use. I always stiffen at his slightest movement, panicked that without warning he's going to yank away my safety net and I'll plummet, the same way I'd done years before whenever he'd pull his hands too soon from my wobbly two-wheeler.

"I'm right *here.*" He's exasperated now. "You could *sit* in this water and not drown, for God's sake! Would I let anything happen to you?"

But each time he withdraws his forearms, I pitch toward the bottom and the familiar panic rises again in my throat.

Finally, my mother's nerves have had enough. She orders us out of the water.

"Dammit, Jenny. If you knew how to swim, you wouldn't *have* to be afraid." My father spews gravel as he backs out of the parking area. "And neither would the kids."

It's the same thing he says every time we go to a beach, but then, he's the only one in our little family who can swim.

My mother doesn't answer. When they have this conversation, she never does. But wedged in the backseat beside my sister and brother, I can picture her hands clenching and unclenching in her lap—white, pink, white, pink, as rhythmic as the rubbery slap of our Chevy's tires on the hot pavement.

"Half your family has some damned water phobia, and look at what it's done to your kids."

I lay in bed sleepless that night after I almost drowned, puzzling over the sight of my father running from the trees.

I'd been completely underwater. So—how? How could I possibly have *seen* him—*heard* him—rushing into the water to save me when I was floating, floating, floating in all that gray?

I hadn't been comfortable near the water for as long as I could remember. Late one summer night about eight years earlier, when I was five or six, friends of my parents, excited about their new speedboat, picked us up on the spur of the moment to go see it. We drove, it seemed, forever, and I fell asleep slumped against my sister in the backseat before we finally stretched out of their station wagon into a starless night. I could see only a small patch of parking lot before the ground fell away in front of us. I held my breath and clutched my mother's hand as I clambered onto the wooden pier in the pitch darkness, too terrified to peer between the planks to where the water lapped below.

"She's a beaut, all right," my father told his friend Blake. I could hear pride and admiration in the adult voices, but I could barely make out the small covered sailboat bobbing in the murky, wavery shadows.

"Where are we?" I asked, still gripping Mama's hand for dear life.

Her blond friend Frieda exhaled a stream of cigarette smoke and patted me on the head. "At the end of the world, honey," she said with the faintest of smiles and without ever taking her eyes off the boat. My breath caught.

At the end of the world!

Awed, I looked a few steps behind me at the station wagon in the tiny parking lot, then turned back to peer past the speedboat, bobbing just beyond. I squinted as hard as I could and saw nothing in the distance but a rolling black abyss. "Really?"

"Oh, you bet," she sighed, still smiling.

I stared past her cigarette smoke and into the abyss, and in the summer heat I shivered—and I believed her.

For years I was convinced we had taken a late night drive to the end of the world, and every time I recalled it, I shuddered at that image of land dropping abruptly away into inky, endless water.

Believing, as children do, that what grown-ups said was the truth.

Chapter One ❧

If not for her father's passport, defaced but not destroyed, Francesca never would have surfaced. She would have remained a woman lost to history, her story swallowed in the depths of the Detroit River off Belle Isle.

The passport was issued in 1914, during the reign of King Vittorio Emanuele III, just fifty-three years after the patriot soldier Giuseppe Garibaldi led the resurgence that unified a patchwork of city-states into a country called Italy. My family left Italy for America with a single passport. Issued to my great-grandfather, it included my great-grandmother and their children, listed in birth order on its inside pages. It was a time when women and children were considered a man's property, when he expected his bride to be a virgin, and their blood-stained wedding sheets were hung in the living room to prove it. It was a time when, married or single, many Italian men openly eschewed monogamy, but a family's honor was bound up in the chastity of its women.

I saw the passport only once, in 1993, but the secret ancestor it had concealed for nearly eighty years instantly became my obsession. I'd had no inkling that my great-aunt Frances had ever existed. She was a blank.

In many families there are secrets. In Italian families, generations go to their graves without divulging those secrets. My mother had never breathed a word about her mother's ill-fated sister Frances, not even to my father. Despite their forty years together as soul mates, he died without ever hearing a whisper of the scandal.

Obsessed, yet fearful of family reprisals for searching out their secret, I fought to piece together my great-aunt's story. A guarded snippet was divulged here, a reluctant dribble there, then *basta!* no more. At times my mother's and her sisters' and their cousins' resistance seemed impregnable, made worse because I needed them as go-betweens to Frances's siblings—their parents. I could no more force myself to press my grandmother on a subject that caused her so much pain than I could force myself to obey my mother and "let it go!" In the face of my own escalating horror, I remained fixated on ferreting out the truth about Frances's life.

She haunted me.

Detroit, 1980s and 1990s

My search for my family's history had begun seven years before I learned of Frances. In the late eighties, on my third trip to Israel, I discovered that Tintori was also a Jewish name. Abraham ben Chayyim dei Tintori, or Abraham the Dyer, was an early printer of Hebrew incunabula who worked in Bologna.

My grandpa Tintori had come to Illinois from the mountains near Bologna to mine coal, and I began searching for twigs on his family tree to learn about the grandfather I'd never known. While I was researching the Tintoris, I decided I should begin to collect information about the Mazzarino side of the family as well. One of the first dictums of genealogy is to sit down with the oldest living relative and ask as many questions about the family as you can, as many times and in as many different ways as possible. My oldest, closest relatives on the Tintori side were long dead when I began their genealogy. I decided I'd better grab Gramma Mazzarino while I could.

One week while she was staying with my mother, I asked my grandmother if I could ask her some questions about her life as a little girl in Sicily, about her parents and grandparents and their history. I already knew a lot, about the voyage to America, the story of her engagement rings, and how the Mafia stepped in to save her wedding. I knew her sisters and brothers and their children well enough, had visited at their homes and spent holidays, weddings, and funerals with them.

"I already told your cousin Claire," she told me. "Go ask her. She's got it all on the tape."

Claire had no idea what I was talking about. She'd interviewed Grandpa Mazzarino for a short biography when she was in sixth grade, but she'd never asked Gramma about her girlhood in Sicily, let alone taped it.

I went back to Gramma, who remained adamant. "Claire, she's got it on the tape. Go ask her."

Thinking perhaps my grandmother had gotten my cousins confused, I asked around. No one had Gramma on tape, audio or video. The tape didn't exist.

"You know, all Gramma and Grandpa's papers are in Aunt Grace's basement," my mother told me, when I mentioned that I would have to write letters to the various *comunes* in Italy and pay for the family birth certificates and marriage licenses. "Before you go spending money, ask your Aunt Grace what Gramma's got there."

I asked. Grace told me. The papers were somewhere in the basement, she didn't know where exactly, but there were naturalization papers, birth certificates, that sort of thing. I asked her to search for them, if she didn't mind. I wanted to make photocopies of them for my genealogy research.

Years went by as I continued researching the Tintoris and my grandfather's survival of the Cherry Mine disaster, and I kept asking Aunt Grace about that box of papers in her basement. Sometimes she'd make a date with me for an afternoon the next time Gramma would be staying with her for a week. Each time, she came up with another excuse for breaking the date.

My mother went through widowhood, a courtship, an engagement, and a remarriage, and still, no matter how many times I asked, I was no further ahead in my Mazzarino research.

Suddenly, when my grandmother was eighty-nine, she relented. She would be staying with my mother and her husband during Christmas week. She would answer my questions about her life in Sicily while I videotaped it.

On Christmas Eve, 1990, I set up my tripod in my mother's kitchen and began to ask about my grandmother's life in Sicily. Two hours later, when I shut down so they could get ready for a Christmas Eve party, my reluctant interviewee had become a ham. Gramma asked when we could do it again.

We never did. She was only at my mother's every third week, I was caught up in family, career, and volunteerism—and I thought I had all the information I needed.

It would take me three more years to get my hands on those papers of hers, though, and a decade longer to unravel the truth about Aunt Frances.

Detroit, 1993

It is a Tuesday morning in the summer of 1993, and *finally* I am in the same room with the Mazzarino family documents—my youngest aunt's kitchen. I almost want to pinch myself, for, even as I was parking, I'd had visions of Grace apologizing as she told me she hadn't found them after all.

"Here's my grandfather's passport," she says, lifting a worn, faded booklet from the musty box she'd set on her kitchen table. I've just rounded that table to kiss my grandmother, who sits running her fingers up and down the handle of her coffee cup.

Aunt Grace sidles alongside me, opening the passport to an inside page, and I glance over at a handwritten list of familiar names—my great-grandmother's, Gramma's, and her siblings'. Jabbing a pearl-polished fingernail at the one entry that had been obliterated from the long list with a pen, Grace breaks the silence. "That's the one they got rid of. Did your mother ever tell you?"

My head jerks back reflexively, as if she'd thrown water in my face, and for a moment I cannot move, cannot speak, my eyes wide with shock.

"Never mind," Grace says, snapping the booklet closed with the realization that my mother had never told me anything.

"Who's she going to show? Who's she going to tell? What's she going to do with these?" Gramma Mazzarino begins to babble in Sicilian, her voice rising in panic with every question. Stupefied, I look down on the back of my grandmother's head, now glowing pink through her fluff of white hair. Her ears glow bright red with agitation.

"Gracie!" she shouts. "What's she going to do with these? People can get hurt!"

I close my ears to my grandmother's sputtering, relieved that our eyes cannot meet, because if they do, I know that I will never again have the chance to get my hands on these papers that have taken years of requests and canceled appointments to pin down. I don't know which I want more—to grab Grace and demand that she explain or to snatch the box of documents from the table and bolt for my car.

"Aunt Grace. What are you talking about?"

She looks away. "Never mind." She is replacing the papers atop a pile jumbled inside a worn cardboard shoe box. "Your mother will tell you." I am dismissed.

Grace turns to silence her own mother, who has not stopped sputtering in Sicilian.

"*Nobody*, Ma! Okay? Nobody else is going to see them. She's just going to go make copies of them for herself and then she's bringing them right back here."

I am unable to wrap my head around what is going on in this kitchen. I want to stamp my foot and silence my grandmother and force my aunt to finish what she's started.

Suddenly I flash on Gramma's repeated refusal to sit with my tape recorder and recount the stories of her childhood. Her insistence, time and again, that I didn't need to preserve her oral history because a tape of it already existed.

"Aunt Grace, you can't do this to me." I round the oval table to follow her now to the sink. "What 'one they got rid of'?"

Now it is Grace's turn to be agitated. She fidgets a dishrag across the counter, swiping at imaginary crumbs. Her tone turns clipped, final.

"You have to ask your mother. I thought she already told you."

"If she didn't tell me by *now,* she's not *going* to. Tell me!"

The dilemma she's spawned is twisting all over Grace's face. Her mother is clamoring for her to drop the subject I'm pressing her to finish. I stare at her, she stares back. She throws down the dishrag.

"That's the one they murdered. Frances. The next sister after Gramma."

My mind flips back and forth because what she's saying is impossible. I know my own grandmother's family. Six boys and three girls, and I know the girls the best. My grandmother is the eldest daughter. When they left Italy, crammed into steerage on the steamer, she took care of all her younger siblings because her mother was pregnant and seasick the entire voyage. Her sisters were Maria, who died of breast cancer when I was a little girl, and Agata, who always wore a scowl as black as her mourning garb, even to my bridal shower. How could there possibly have been another sister? A sister I'd never heard a thing about?

Gramma Mazzarino worries her hand across the clear plastic cover protecting Grace's ecru lace tablecloth. A fine sheen of sweat has blossomed on her reddened face and neck, dampening the hair at her nape. I look away. This is impossible for me to comprehend.

She had a sister who was murdered?

Detroit, 1995

On the morning of Gramma Mazzarino's funeral, a framed 8×10 photograph was sneaked onto a side table near her casket. It went unnoticed by me—by most mourners—since for three days the viewing room had been jammed with people, flowers, and the numerous photos on display as a pictorial essay of my grandmother's life.

As we exited our cars at the cemetery, my cousin Anthony came rushing over to me, his eyes wide with astonishment. Like his sisters, he knew the paltry bits and pieces I'd managed to gather about Francesca—I'd told them.

"Did you see the picture?" he breathed. He didn't have to say another word. Instinctively, I knew exactly whose picture and how it got there. We had heard that only one photograph of her had survived, but no one of our generation had ever seen it. His mother, Grace, must have quietly brought Frances to her elder sister's funeral.

"Where?"

"My ma took it off the credenza next to the casket. Grandma and Grandpa's wedding picture. It's in the trunk of my parents' car."

I knew my grandparents' wedding picture. They were the only two people in it.

I tracked down my aunt the minute we arrived at the postburial luncheon, and asked her for the photo. She feigned ignorance, then waved me off, claiming to have no idea where it was. Realizing it was then or never, I scoured the throng of friends and relatives for her husband.

"Uncle Sam, may I borrow your car keys for a second? There's something I need to get from your trunk."

Alone in the parking lot that October afternoon, I popped open their trunk and took a deep breath. And then I turned over the facedown picture frame and met Gramma's hidden sister for the first time.

. . .

Light glowing from her face and a huge floppy bow tying back her long hair, Frances peeked out at me in black and white from my grandparents' wedding portrait. Unlike the hand-colored portrait of my grandparents in their Sunday best that my mother had always told me was her parents' wedding photo, this one showed my twenty-five-year-old grandfather Nino Mazzarino sporting a proper tuxedo and boutonniere and my fifteen-year-old grandmother Giuseppina, sitting frothed in bridal gown and veil balancing an armload of jumbo mums. Sandwiched between them stand Frances and another of the younger sisters, Mary.

The play of light across the black-and-white portrait consistently pulls the eye to Frances's small face. Her expression keeps me there. With a direct and open gaze, she peers at me across time like a lovely little ghost. Her eyes are large and round and penetrating. Oval and sweet, her face is demure, almost wistful, so young and so innocent.

She is captured on film on the brink of womanhood, frozen forever in September 1916. She is two years removed from Sicily and two years younger than the elder sister who on that day had married for love.

That day I stood staring at thirteen-year-old Frances with my heart pounding. She compelled me to hunt down her story. She still does.

Staring at that photograph now, jewel-framed on my desk, I wonder: Did you already know your barber then, Frances? Were you dreaming about him at the Holy Family Church as the priest blessed your sister's marriage? Were you lost in fantasies that morning, daydreaming of a wedding of your own?

I can picture Frances later on that warm fall afternoon, giggling with her sisters and female cousins at Josie and Nino's wedding feast, smiling shyly at her young barber from across her parents' backyard. She answers the other girls' conversation but her eyes are only for him. Watching as, jacket flying, he dances the tarantella. Watching as, fingers flying, he vies with her brothers along the rose-covered fence in a raucous game of *morra*, all the while pretending not to notice that her eyes are on him.

Dutifully, she would have spent the previous two days helping the women cook and clean and prepare for the wedding, and perhaps, amidst the preparations, one of them teased Frances—the next daughter—about a match with her son. But this was not Palermo, she was in America now. While maintaining a respectful silence to this *cummari*, this "godmother," honorary or actual, her round dark eyes flash emphatically to her mother—"NO!" She had already chosen for herself, with her heart—and without a clue to the consequences.

Frances's story is one my mother never wanted me to know or to tell. It spans two continents, three centuries, and four generations—my great-grandmother's, my grandmother's and her sister Frances's, my mother's, and mine.

It is a story about what mothers owe their daughters and what daughters owe their mothers.

In 1920 Francesca Costa was sixteen and she was in love. Straddling two cultures and the turn of a century, she stood at the threshold of a vibrant, exciting future. Possibilities and freedoms that none of her female ancestors in Italy could have even fantasized about shimmered on her horizon. She was in America, where she saw young women choosing their own spouses, marrying for love instead of duty. They wore short kicky skirts, sleeveless dresses, and cropped hairdos. American women had a voice, one about to become more powerful when they won the right to vote on August 18 of that year.

But like Shakespeare's Juliet, Frances embraced a forbidden love and not the one her father had forced upon her. Her duty was to remain chaste, compliant, obedient, and silent, to forget her heart and accept the handpicked suitor that her father, like Juliet's, had invited to look her over like a piece of property for purchase. But Frances and her barber proved more than star-crossed lovers. In life as in fiction, these young people fell tragic victims to their society, in which a woman's sexuality was governed by her male relatives, who placed more value on her maidenhead than on her head—or on her heart.

Frances's story begins in Sicily, an island fixed at the crossroads of civilization. Lying between Italy and Africa, almost exactly in the middle of the Mediterranean Sea, Sicily is separated from the toe of Italy's boot by the narrow Strait of Messina, and from Africa by less than eighty-seven miles of water. Not quite a quarter the size of Cuba, its strategic importance and a history of plunder stand disproportionately to its size. Seismic activity beneath the island mimics its volatile history. The island has never stopped seething—and as recently as 150 years ago, a tiny land mass claimed by Sicily briefly poked its face at the sun just off the mother island before ducking underwater once more.

On a March morning in 1914, Frances's family said good-bye to their relatives and left Palermo for Naples, on the Italian mainland, where the steamship that would speed them away from misery waited. It was the last time six of these eight Costas would ever again set foot in Sicily.

Two days later, Domenico Costa shepherded his pregnant wife, Concetta, and their six younger children, Giuseppina, Francesca, Agata, Maria, Luigi, and Salvatore, into the bowels of the giant ship and set sail for a better life in America.

Chapter Two ❧

On·the Atlantic Ocean, 1914

By the third day at sea, the Costa children's unbounded elation about their voyage to l'America was a distant memory. Were it an option, they'd have happily jumped into the icy March sea and swum back to Palermo. From the minute they'd walked down the stairs into the steerage compartment designated for families (women traveling alone had their own stairs and segregated compartment, as did solo men) their stomachs had roiled at the odors hanging in those dank, close quarters. The wooden deck reeked from the absorbed vomit of a thousand voyages, and the stale air stank from the lingering odors of tens of thousands of unwashed bodies. Regulations called for a foot-square ventilation shaft for every fifty passengers, but few steamship lines complied. Eight months pregnant, their mother, Concetta, was well beyond bouts of morning sickness, yet she had retched up her meager breakfast before she even reached the bunks assigned to her family.

While waiting in line for the doctor to administer vaccinations before they could board the ship, their patriarch, Domenico, had warned his family that space on board would be tight. Still, Concetta and the children were unprepared for these cramped quarters. The berths, stacked like bunk beds, were six feet long by two feet wide, outfitted with a short thin blanket set over a mattress and a pillow filled with straw and covered in coarse white canvas. With just thirty inches of open space above each mattress, it was impossible for anyone but a child to sit up in bed, yet no chairs were provided for the adults.

All around them the deck reverberated with the commotion and complaints of hundreds of other families lugging their belongings, finding their allotted spaces, and settling in. Domenico, a veteran of several Atlantic crossings, ordered the older children into the upper berths and showed them how to stand on the iron rails of the bottom bed in order to hoist themselves or their belongings up top. He took a top bunk for himself and directed Concetta and the little ones into the lower beds. Then he began shoving the family's satchels and boxes into the berths.

"Domenico! What are you thinking?" Concetta cried, as she removed her shawl. "Put those under the beds."

"They allow nothing on the floor, not even underneath. Everything goes in the beds."

"Where is there any room for me to sleep?" Francesca complained, drawing up her feet as her father moved her life preserver aside to sling yet another satchel onto the foot of her bed.

"Where are the hooks for our clothes?" Concetta asked, looking around their small quarters for a space to hang them.

"Everything goes in the beds," Domenico repeated. "Besides, there's not enough privacy for changing."

Concetta spotted the long board attached to the wall, narrow and waist high, and moved to lay her shawl there.

"That is where we eat," Domenico told her. "There, or in the beds."

Luigi buried his nose in Concetta's belly. "Why does it smell so bad in here, Mama?"

"When it doesn't rain, we go up top for fresh air," Domenico told his family. "Most of the people do, so it is hard to find room to stand out there, but we can try."

"I need to pee," Agata whined.

"Giuseppina, take her to the toilets," Domenico told her. He pointed toward a crew member. "Ask the signore where to find them."

"I have to go, too." Francesca jumped out of her bunk, ready to explore.

"And then I want you immediately back here," Concetta told them.

The steward directed them up the flight of stairs, then told them to walk halfway down the top deck where they would certainly find the women's bathroom by the line already formed outside it. Once inside, instead of a ceramic pot like the one they used at home, the girls discovered that the toilet room's six short and narrow stalls sheltered only open floor troughs, which were already filthy. They saw iron handles affixed to the side walls of the stalls, which they soon learned were important to hang on to while squatting at sea. The washroom was separate, with women and girls and little boys—and sometimes men—crowded around the ten deep sinks that lined two walls of the seven-by-nine-foot room. This, they learned, was the only place where they would be able to wash themselves, their dishes, and their clothing. Each sink had two faucets, something the girls had never seen before. Imitating the woman to her left, Francesca turned the handle on one faucet but nothing came out. When she tried the other, it spat out a stream of icy salt water. There was no soap, and there were no towels, so the girls wiped their hands on their skirts and meandered back to the family, gaping at everything and everyone along the way.

They squeezed past people jabbering in languages they could not understand, although some of them sounded vaguely like their own. They spotted a snack bar where some women were already buying fresh apples and plums, and another bar crowded with men drinking from small glasses. Near their berths they discovered a small area outfitted with several unusual tables that had long seats built right onto them. These narrow boards, which could seat six or seven people, were attached to the framework extending from each long side of the table, but the girls couldn't imagine how they might maneuver themselves over the boards and into those seats with their long skirts.

As they neared the family berths, the girls heard a clanging racket rising above the din of voices. The closer they got, the louder it sounded until they saw that the noise was coming from their own berths. Luigi, four, and Salvatore, two, were sitting beside their mother, banging away on large tin pots.

"What do they have?" Agata asked, running over to inspect her brothers' makeshift toys.

"Put those lunch pails away already and make sure they don't lose the forks and spoons," Domenico said. "These are the only dishes and eating utensils each of us is going to get, and everyone must rinse them off and put them right back into their bed after every meal, *capiddu?* Otherwise, you'll have to eat with your hands until we get to America."

The talk of food roiled Concetta's stomach once again, but when she vomited onto the floor this time, Francesca became sick as well. Mortified, Concetta looked around for something to clean the floor.

"There's nothing you can do," Domenico told her. "Just leave it. The stewards come twice a day to sweep the floor, once in the morning before the captain comes around for inspection, and once late in the day to sweep aside the apple cores and plum pits and the garbage and vomit. Then they'll try to sell you some hard-cooked eggs or apples."

It was an irony that Concetta and her children—in fact, most of the passengers in steerage—were nauseated throughout this voyage and unable to stomach much food at a time when food was more plentiful than it had been during their entire lifetimes. Still, at the first sign of the stewards' mealtime activity, everyone who was able rushed from their berth to line up with their meal pail. The recipes were uninspired, the quality of the food was at best only fair, but at least there was always bread and something to drink.

Those who could read were able to report the menus posted on the compartment walls. A breakfast of bread and butter, oatmeal—something the Costas had never seen before—a protein like cheese, corned beef, or herring, and coffee with milk and sugar, was served at seven in the morning. Dinner, the main meal, served midday, offered a daily variety: some sort of hearty soup containing vegetables, a portion of meat, and potatoes or pudding with plum sauce. At three in the afternoon, the stewards brought out coffee and bread or cake. For supper they dished up rice or barley cooked in warm milk with plums, or Irish stew or a ragout, served with rye bread and butter and hot tea with sugar. The food was plentiful. Every day Giuseppina and Francesca watched as the leftovers were dumped into the sea.

After meals the women thronged the washroom sinks in an attempt to rinse the grease and food from their families' rusty plates and utensils with the cold sea water. It was even less possible to wash themselves. The steerage passengers were living on top of one another with no walls or partitions and the washrooms and toilets were continuously filled beyond capacity, precluding even a modicum of privacy. With no one ever donning sleeping attire or exchanging their soiled or sweat-stained clothing for clean garments, early into the voyage various body oil and sweat odors began to waft amid the smell of seasickness.

Of the entire family, Giuseppina was the only Costa who had a sturdy stomach. She would often tell her grandchildren the story of their rough voyage to America. Just thirteen, she realized she had to take care of her seasick parents and siblings. As early as possible each day, usually as the other passengers began to rouse at five in the morning, she hurried to shepherd her younger siblings up onto one of the two upper decks to stand and escape the foul cabin. There, she constantly had to coax Luigi and Salvatore away from the railings, where they ran so they could watch the sea rush by. The fresh air revived the children, leaving Giuseppina to rein in their curiosity and exuberance each time they began to clamber onto the equipment and machinery seeking someplace to sit, since there were no deck chairs or benches. After listening to women's cries as crew members mingled among the passengers on deck, she enlisted Francesca's help in keeping her siblings away from the crew's nasty hands. She'd overheard enough in the women's wash-room to know that the crew passed up no opportunity to prey upon the single women travelers aboard. She heard enough on the decks to know that many of the men were crude and their language re-volting, and when she spied them, she steered her little family out of earshot.

Cinders were another constant annoyance, raining from the smokestacks to bite the passengers' eyes and blanket their hair and clothing. They fell so thickly that two stewards kept their brooms constantly employed, sweeping them into the sea. By eight each night, these same two shooed everyone below so that they could pull down the huge hoses and wash off the open decks.

Though Giuseppina marched her brothers and sisters to the washroom daily and cleaned them up as best she could, the facili-ties were so awash in water that her littlest brothers were more in-tent on splashing and stomping in the overflow that swirled around their shoes. She faithfully hung their few towels across the metal frame at the side of the bunks, hoping they would dry. They never did. With four hundred or so people crammed into the steer-age compartment there was little room left for air to circulate.

Although the ship's doctor and an officer were supposed to in-spect the passengers daily, their routine was haphazard. Every few days the two would line up the passengers, glance them over, and automatically fill in the missing days' checkmarks on their cards. Once each day, when the captain posted the distance they had traveled, Giuseppina would check the notice and report the progress to encourage her wobbly family. Finally, after two weeks at sea, Giuseppina and Francesca came running to announce that l'America was just a day away.

Suddenly there was a flurry of activity among the stewards. Washrooms and toilets were cleaned for the first time since the ship pulled away from Palermo. The doctor and officer made one last health inspection, checking everyone's arm for vaccination, then completed the checkmarks on every passenger's card. Cheered by their proximity to land, the weary travelers summoned the strength to clean themselves somewhat before arrival. Concetta joined the other mothers standing at the washbasins scrubbing the heads of their squealing children in icy water. With her two eldest girls' help, she repacked their satchels, tucking in the parting gifts the stewards had distributed to their passengers—some candies for the women and a pipe and tobacco for the men.

Word spread quickly through the cabin that land was in sight, and the Costas followed the tangle of passengers dashing for the open deck and their first glimpse of America. When the lights of America glittered before them, Francesca and her older sister, Giuseppina, stood next to their mother with their mouths agape, intoxicated by the sight. Nothing they'd ever seen could have prepared them for this vision. So many lights, as if the stars had settled on the horizon in clusters!

The Costa family stood on deck watching as the lights grew brighter and closer, until the stewards ordered all passengers back to their berths. The ship would not approach the Statue of Liberty until morning, they assured them, and then still had to make its way two hundred miles inland to reach Marcus Hook, where state and federal inspectors waited to clear them for arrival in Philadelphia.

Gramma Mazzarino told me that her first sight of the New York harbor and the Statue of Liberty was the most wondrous thing she saw in her entire lifetime. She was only thirteen, Francesca just ten, but the sisters' young hearts were so full of anticipation they hurt. Who could have imagined such a place? They wondered if Detroit was that beautiful, too.

In Philadelphia, the Costas would have to pass another medical examination. They would also have to correctly answer a barrage of questions before federal inspectors released them to the ticket office where they could book their travel into Detroit. Domenico readied his passport, which also listed his wife and the children accompanying them from Sicily, and ordered Concetta not to speak unless an inspector addressed her directly. The children knew better than to utter a whimper, terrified that a single mis-

take could find them back on that horrible ship, most likely returning to Sicily all alone, which happened frequently. Concetta's
job was to pinch the children's cheeks to brighten their pallid faces
with the rosiness of health. Domenico's was to take care of all the
talking, through the assigned interpreter.

The tang of seawater in the air revived Concetta, but she was
weary of traveling. She could not wait to reach Detroit and scrub
the memories of this wretched journey from her family's hair and
clothing. With her children sprawled across satchels at her feet,
she sat on a carton in the train station and rubbed her abdomen to
quiet the restless one within. Her little unborn *'Medicano* was going to have a beautiful life, full of hope and possibility. They all
were.

Chapter Three ❧

Corleone, Sicily, 1903

Francesca was born the fifth and prettiest of my great-grandparents' ten children. Unlike her older siblings, born in nearby Partinico during the final decade of the 1800s, Francesca was the first of Domenico and Concetta's children to be born in Corleone—and in the new century.

Domenico may have cursed her arrival—*My wife now can only produce useless girls!*—wanting instead for Concetta to deliver another brother for Rocco, Pasquale, and Angelo, the three young sons who preceded their first daughter, two-year-old Giuseppina. The hands of sons brought money into a peasant family. The hands of daughters took it away.

At the same time Henry Ford was incorporating in Detroit, the feudal system was still solidly rooted in the Sicilian soil despite the dissolution of the land barons' grand estates following the unification of Italy nearly four decades earlier. Only the boys could lend their muscles to providing food for the family table by working the land, even if the parcel they tilled was no more than a small vegetable plot near home. Francesca, her sister Giuseppina, and every other girl in Sicily, would be good only to help their mothers get that food to the table, using their hands for washing and baking and cleaning and cooking. Each day, when that work was finished, they would sit outside until nightfall bent over their looms, flurrying their fingers over shuttles and threads, humming and singing while they worked. Facing the house, never the street, the young females would spend long hours weaving the fabric they would sew into the family's clothing and bedding and curtains.

Daughters were a burden on the impoverished Sicilian peasants, not only because they could not bolster the family income, but because each one cost her family a *corredo*, the dowry they were hard-pressed to come by. *Bambine nelle fascie, biancheria nella cascia*, the Sicilians said—"Swaddling clothes on the baby girl, white ware in her hope chest."

Young women from destitute families often remained unwed since every Sicilian bride was required to bring twelve sets of "beds" to her marriage, six heavy ones for winter and six light ones for summer. Each bed, or *letto*, consisted of two sheets, four pillowcases, a bedspread, lingerie for the bride, towels, tablecloths, napkins, and doilies, and cost a fortune in thread. The skill with which a young *ragazza* wove and stitched them was the mark of the girl's worth as a catch. The more *letti* she produced, and the more elaborately laced and decorated she embroidered them, the more prized she became as a prospective fiancée. For this reason, girls from wealthy families often stacked up to twenty-four sets of *letti* in their wooden *cassete*—hope chests—by hiring out the weaving and stitching of those extra "beds" to peasant women.

While the handwork was done by the daughter, her fathers and brothers had to toil for the means to purchase the materials she needed to create a proper *corredo*. When asked how many children he had, many a *Siciliano* would automatically reply that he had fathered X number of sons and X number of "burdens."

As Sicilian men began emigrating to America in desperation to find work, the dowry situation worsened at home. Working at the most menial of jobs, the men were merely subsisting in America and sending the bulk of their earnings back to their "white widows," who were likewise scraping by in their Sicilian villages. Many men abandoned their families and Sicily permanently, embarking on new lives with new families across the ocean. With their fathers gone for stretches of one to three years—sometimes more, and sometimes forever—many a *ragazza* of marriageable age sat husbandless for lack of a proper *corredo*.

Partinico, where Francesca was conceived in 1903, was among Sicily's poorest towns. There were no yards there, no sidewalks. Stone walls of houses and buildings grew straight up from its streets. Had Francesca's father been able to see into the future, he'd have known that his decision to leave Partinico was the right one, for as many as fifty years later it remained one of the poorest agricultural communities in Sicily, with unpaved roads, illiteracy, barefoot kids, and destitution at every door.

With his fifth child on the way and no chance of finding work, Domenico had gathered his pregnant Concetta, their children, their chickens, their donkey, and their meager possessions, and abandoned their hovel in Partinico for another like it in Corleone. But the poverty had followed—or had stretched ahead of them— like their own shadows.

Set inland about thirty-five miles south of Palermo in a hollow between Monti Sicani's peaks, Corleone is small even now, a hilly home to just eleven thousand. Surrounding the town proper, bizarrely shaped rocks jut from verdant hills grabbed by the roots of ancient olive groves and dotted with colorful fields of crops. Now infamous, Corleone conjures images of a young Al Pacino, of sun-dappled orange groves and hundreds of churches.

Corleone—a derivation of Kurlion, a name from Sicily's Arabic past—was agricultural and as fertile as Concetta, whose twenty-two pregnancies in twenty years produced eleven live births but only ten children who would live past infancy. If the land there could produce, perhaps, Domenico thought, he could likewise provide for his family.

When Francesca was born, it was the custom for Italians to herald the birth of a child with wine. The men downed three glasses to welcome a son and two glasses for a daughter, tempering the latter celebration because females were "born to suffering." But Francesca's arrival was not toasted at all. In October 1903 the Costa family had no money for food, let alone for wine.

That afternoon Domenico walked to the Corleone town hall with his brother, Mario, to attest to his second daughter's arrival. He couldn't read the fancy script of the clerk who registered at his dictation the live birth that day of Francesca Costa to Domenico Costa and Concetta Lupica.

The day after Francesca was born, Concetta was back at her housewifely duties. She began her day by pulling on her dark-blue-and-white-checked dimity bodice and the blue-and-white-striped skirt, both of which she'd woven. Slipping her blue-stockinged feet into pointy-toed, low-heeled calfskin slippers, she tied on her dark striped apron even as she hurried to change Francesca's swaddling cloths. For protection, she tucked saints' pictures between the strips of cloth as she tightly rewrapped the infant from her shoulders to her ankles. During the three days until the infant's soul would be redeemed by baptism, Concetta would neither kiss Francesca nor begin to bond with the tiny "pagan," for Sicilians considered their newborns soulless "Turks," and mothers held their newborns only to suckle them.

After she set Francesca down on her back on the wool pillow she used for carrying her, Concetta set to sweeping animal waste from the mud floor of their compact home and then left to carry the family toilet away to dump it near the outskirts of town.

Three days later, after she'd cleared away the breakfast crumbs, she dressed her other children in their least worn clothes and took Giuseppina outside the front door to brush the snarls from her curly hair. Last, she brushed out her own long brown hair and wrapped it into a tight knot at the nape of her neck. By the time Concetta had everyone else readied, the midwife who had delivered Francesca arrived and the two women turned their attention to preparing the little pagan for her day of entry into the Catholic Church. Concetta took from her hope chest, the painted wooden *casa de noce,* the embroidered white baptismal gown provided by Francesca's godparents, and pulled it over the swaddled infant. Then the midwife tied three tiny caps onto Francesca's head, placed her on her carrying pillow, and handed her off to her god-mother for the procession to church. Waving to the neighbors who showered blessings on little Francesca that Sunday, the procession of Costas, midwife, and godparents walked the little one to the small church nearby.

There, the *cummari* ("co-mother") and the *cumpari* ("co-father") carried the infant inside to the parish priest and swore they would stand as her spiritual guardians, denouncing Satan and requesting admission to the Church on her behalf. Then they handed Francesca back to the midwife to hold during the ceremony to symbolize her second, spiritual, birth. Pouring holy water on the infant's head and calling on the Father, the Son, and the Holy Ghost, the *padre* baptized her Francesca after Concetta's mother, as is the Italian custom. Every first daughter is named after her fa-ther's mother, the second daughter for her mother's mother; each first son is named after his father's father, the second son for his mother's father; all subsequent children are named however their parents wish. The infant mortality in Italy was high, so the name of a child called after a grandparent did not die with that child. Some mothers buried several Giovannis or Marias before the appropriate grandparent was duly honored with a living namesake.

To Italians, their children's godparents are the highest ranked of their numerous relatives and friends. Chosen from among the parents' closest friends and relatives, the *cummari*'s and *cumpari*'s status as guardians of the infant's soul binds them to that child and to its parents in a special relationship that transforms friend-ship into blood kinship and double-knots preexisting familial ties. Children called their godparents by the special names *padrino* and *padrina,* which echo the word for father, *padre,* and accords them for life the utmost affection and respect. So close was the tie of *cummari/cumpari* relationships in Sicily that men who had reconciled after a dispute would vow to seal the bond by becoming *cumparis* as soon as one of them had another child.

Five days after Francesca was born, right after breakfast, Domenico picked up his wooden dance pallet instead of his work tools and announced that he was heading off to compete in a series of dance contests in other towns up and down the countryside. He prided himself on being an excellent dancer who often took the prize purse for first place. On this warm October morning, Domenico left his home filled with anticipation. He was looking forward to days away from his bleeding wife and bawling infant, to dancing on tabletops to the cheers of an audience, and to the beds of any women he was certain to charm with his fancy footwork. These days he made sure there was some food in the house when his feet were itching. Once, when they had only the three eldest boys, Domenico had taken off without a word to Concetta. After two days with no food and no husband, she called on his brother, Mario, to plead for something to feed her children. Mario watched for his brother's return and met him at the door the following evening with fists flying.

"You think it's right to leave your wife and three babies with no food in the house for three days while you go have a good time, you damn fool?" he panted between punches. "You think this is right?"

Chapter Four ❧

Detroit, 1914

From the moment they stepped off the train and into the towering, grand Michigan Central Station, Giuseppina, Francesca, and their siblings walked around dumbfounded by the startling sights and uncommon sounds of America. As they crossed the cavernous terminal, craning their necks to gape at the three-story-high ceiling, Domenico told his family that this station had been built just the year before. Never had they been inside a building as beautiful or as large, nor one with such elegant arched windows. Even the cathedral in Palermo seemed smaller by comparison, Concetta decided.

Her older sister Rosalia had recently immigrated to Detroit with her husband, but to Concetta, Rosalia was long dead. The grudge she harbored against Rosalia lodged as deep as the betrayal and hurt that had spawned it. Since Concetta would have nothing to do with her sister, Domenico moved his family into the house of a *cumpari*, a close family friend who lived on Rivard Street, less than a half mile from Detroit's riverfront. Most every newcomer settled with established *cumparis* until they could afford to move into their own homes. Concetta was grateful for the small enclave of Sicilians situated in this neighborhood, which eased the stress of transition to their new home. There was already too much to acclimate themselves to, and now they had to negotiate living space with another large family. That their sensory environment was still Sicilian—with the language, cooking aromas, and customs of home—proved comforting.

Detroit was a huge, dizzying, and, unlike Corleone, very flat city. Domenico reported that he'd yet to find a hill in any of its twenty-three square miles. En route to their new home, Francesca and her siblings and mother were astonished by the bustle of traffic in the city. There were trolley cars hooked to a web of electrical wires that stretched across the sky, fine carriages pulled by horse teams, and shiny motor cars rumbling down the wide roads. Though she shivered in the crisp spring chill for lack of a coat, at first sight of their new home Francesca shouted that her papa had found them a castle!

The house was nearly identical to every other house lining the block, rising two stories high and made entirely of painted wood, with windows of leaded glass. Trees lined the sidewalks to form a canopy over the street. Manicured patches of grass spread like faded green welcome mats in front and in back, and half of the backyard had been tilled for garden vegetables.

Outside, wide wooden stairs led to porches flanking both the front and back doors. Inside, there was more room than the children could have imagined. One flight of stairs led up to the bedrooms, where sturdy doors with glass-knobbed handles hung in the doorways, while the staircase beneath it snaked into a dark and musty basement that held a coal furnace and a narrow storage pantry. Francesca and her siblings ran to explore the main level, laughing at the clatter their shoes made on the polished wood floors. This floor was divided into several small rooms—the one in front reserved for sitting, the middle one for eating, and a separate kitchen at the back. One wall was lined with wooden cupboards, a strange black metal stove, and a sink set into a counter patterned with small black and white tiles identical to those covering the floor.

This roomy, exotic house had features they never could have imagined, but no sleeping loft like the one they had in Corleone. Instead, the girls spent each night huddled on the floor under the long table in the dining room, while the boys slept in two upstairs bedrooms on blankets spread on the floor. The four parents shared the front bedroom, squashing themselves into a bed built for two, the women sandwiched in the center while the two husbands flanked the outside edges.

Everything about America was strange, my grandmother told me—the houses, the tree-lined streets, the sidewalks, the noisy vehicles—but the *Medicani* were strangest of all. She and Francesca marveled that here females were apparently free to come and go as they pleased, while Concetta and her cronies clucked their tongues at such lack of propriety. Sometimes alone, sometimes in pairs, American women walked unsupervised everywhere at will—to the market, to church, to visit in the neighborhood. They not only rode the streetcars unaccompanied by their men, some of them even maneuvered automobiles down the roads solo. Despite all the stories Papa had recounted about their new country, he had never told them this.

The women in America were fascinating to Giuseppina and Francesca. Like the women in Sicily, they wore long skirts, but their solid-colored shirtwaist blouses were of finer fabrics, buttoned up the front, and underneath them the women wore corsets to cinch in their waists. They always went out in public wearing gloves and something on their heads, usually a hat, and the bigger the better. They wore their hair long, piled atop their heads to emulate the "Gibson Girl," the paragon of beauty immortalized in the sketches of Charles Dana Gibson. Like the other immigrant women, Concetta studied the women's fashions and used her talent with the needle to recreate them for herself and her daughters.

American men were dapper, too. They wore suits and hats to the office and on Sundays. Haircuts were short, and males sported beards and moustaches and shaved with a straight razor after lathering up with a special stubby brush and soap sold in mugs. The Costa boys imitated their father, trimming their hair and moustaches and trading in their stocking caps for proper felt hats.

The Costas wrestled with new ways and a new language.

Domenico's sons brought home English words from the factory, and Agata, Maria, and Luigi brought home more from school. They spoke their newfound English with a Sicilian cadence, their words often ending in a soft *a*. The younger children's palates were still pliable enough to roll out the English words without a trace of an accent. Their American-born descendants would later regard those youngest Costas as truly American, even though Michael was the only one born in the States.

Though Concetta, Giuseppina, and Francesca struggled to mimic the younger ones' precise pronunciations, they couldn't get their tongues around the English words. Their mouths had been Sicilian for too long.

Though most of Detroit's Italian immigrants held jobs at the lowest end of the spectrum—peddlers, sewer diggers, laborers—more than half of them owned their own homes. They'd lived too long on someone else's land as indentured servants under Sicily's feudal system, always in debt and at risk of being booted off a farm, to do otherwise. Here, hard work and scrupulous scrimping could ensure them of a plot of land and a sturdy roof of their own.

To supplement the two dollars the railroad paid him weekly to shovel a half ton of coal, Domenic, as he came to be called in Detroit, played bocce on Sunday afternoons, counting on his usual two- to three-dollar winnings to augment his wages. Within six months, the Costas had moved on to their own home, a wood-frame house on Monroe Street, not far from either Woodward Avenue or La Chiesa della Sacra Famiglia, the Holy Family Church.

Though he was still stuck at the railroad where he'd labored to earn passage for the rest of his family, Domenic's three eldest boys all had jobs with Mr. Ford, and Concetta had given birth to the first American Costa, a boy they named Michael.

While Concetta could not forget the Sicilian proverb she'd known firsthand—"If I had a saucepan, water, and salt, I'd make bread stew. *If* I had bread"—she could now afford to bake more than two loaves of bread each week. But although meat was less costly in America, it remained an infrequently eaten delicacy. Sirloin could be had for twenty-four cents a pound, and chicken or turkey for seven. Canned vegetables cost a dime, but everyone canned fresh fruits and vegetables for the winter, and her *cummaris* taught Concetta the process so she could stock her basement cellar.

Pasta was the staple of their diet and she learned to prepare it with every variety of vegetable. One night it was pasta with cauliflower fried in oil and garlic, another it was pasta with broccoli or with peas and onion or with just tomato. Eggs, at twelve cents a dozen, were another staple, beaten foamy and fried in a large frittata with onion and peas or onion and asparagus and a dusting of Parmesan. As in Sicily, the family still waited until Domenic had eaten his first mouthful to lift their own forks, and Concetta still ate her meal from her husband's plate.

Salt was more plentiful thanks to the vast salt mines tunneled beneath Detroit, and Domenic preferred his food heavily salted. No matter how many times Concetta asked him to leave a portion of the food at her side of the oval plate unsalted, no matter how many times she gagged down her meal, or spat out her complaints, Domenic never entertained a modicum of courtesy. Every meal he salted the entire plate of food, and every meal she opened up her mouth to him until he ordered her to silence. The Costa children learned to eat quickly. Whoever finished first won the sparse leftovers and escape from the constant bickering. In America, their mother had grown less afraid to speak her mind.

Concetta sewed crinolines for Agata and Maria and knickers for Luigi so they could dress like the American children, and every morning she walked the girls to the public school. Giuseppina and Francesca could read and do their numbers, so she kept them at home to help with the cooking, cleaning, marketing, and gardening and to supervise little Luigi, Salvatore, and Michael while she sewed. Housewives boiled the laundry, scrubbed it by hand on ribbed washboards, and hung it outside to dry. And all of it had to be ironed.

While she couldn't read the *Ladies' Home Journal*, Concetta could peruse the illustrations of items for sale in America's "wish book," the Sears, Roebuck Catalogue, which advertised rockers for $2.95 and wood-burning stoves for $17.48. Francesca could read the numbers and told her mother that a woman's skirt cost four dollars, a shirtwaist three dollars, and a man's suit would set him back nine dollars, but Concetta knew she could sew them for a fraction of that. She studied the American styles and duplicated them for her family, and then used her remnants to make aprons, which she sold in the neighborhood. Supervising from a chair on the front porch, Domenic allowed her to take her aprons door to door after dinner, always accompanied by Giuseppina, Francesca, or Agata.

In Sicily, Concetta and her daughters had sat outside facing their house during daylight hours to groom themselves, sew and weave, and visit with the neighbors. In Detroit, sprawl separated them. The streets were wider and the houses were freestanding and set slightly apart, precluding the cozy community conversation of Sicily. With a flight of stairs and a porch railing separating their women from the street, husbands weren't so rigid about them sitting outside with their backs to the world. It would have made it too hard to shout back and forth with a *cummari* who lived on the opposite side of the street.

While families like the Costas found security in their Sicilian enclave, they had no idea they lived in the former houses of judges, novelists, attorneys, steamship and ferry owners, actors, sculptors, painters, and opera stars. Abolitionist John Brown and General U. S. Grant once called this neighborhood home. Now, many Detroiters' lips curled at the mention of Little Sicily, a disdain that further isolated the immigrants and made assimilation harder.

A *Sunday Free Press* article bemoaned the transformation of the elite Detroit neighborhood into a "human anthill" whose olive-skinned race overflowed onto the sidewalks and made a district as picturesque as it was smelly.

"For many years it remained the headquarters of the pushcart brigade," the article continued, "who ripened their stock of bananas in foul cellars and trudged many weary miles every day disposing of the wares that were to bring them the longed-for fortune, while their wives sat on the doorsteps and chattered in a strange tongue and half-dressed bambinas romped on the pavement."

There was a young laborer living in the same neighborhood whose walk to the streetcar often took him past the Costas' house. Antonino Mazzarino had left his birthplace of Mazara del Vallo, a fishing port on the western coast of Sicily, four years earlier when he was nineteen. His departure tortured his mother, Giovannina, because their little family hadn't heard one word from Nino's older brother, Giuseppe, in the two years since he had fled to Argentina to avoid the army. Giovannina was the abandoned wife of a wealthy husband, Nicola, left to support three babies when Nicola's brother-in-law introduced him to a woman of means, suggesting that the two might do well to combine their fortunes. Although Giovannina's family and friends had pressed her to give the children to Nicola and his new wife, she could sooner have given away her heart.

While his father sired three more children who went to school well dressed and with food in their bellies, Nino didn't have a pair of shoes or a hat until he was twelve years old. He was a man before he learned he had siblings from his father's second marriage. No matter how many days he'd stood outside the schoolyard and watched the children laugh at recess, he'd never had a clue that his sister, Angelina, had taken him and Giuseppe there for a glimpse of their younger brothers and sister.

Nino knew who his father was, however, and would cross the street with downcast eyes to avoid speaking to him. When Nino was seventeen, his father's money finally put food on his mother's table. Giuseppe had yet to send the money he had promised upon finding work in Argentina, and Angelina and her mother couldn't even earn a few pennies with their sewing. Left standing jobless in Mazara's town square morning after morning while other peasants were fleeing to America to survive, Nino accepted that he had no other options. He choked down his gall and asked for a job in his father's vineyards.

The boy was adept with a knife and twine and was pleased when plants flourished in his hands. Quickly he became a skilled grafter and his lifelong talent for cultivation took root. Years later, across an ocean, he would grow rosebushes from single blossoms plucked out of his daughters' bridesmaids' bouquets, then stuck in the ground to hibernate for a year inside a mason jar "greenhouse" that he had screwed into the earth.

One afternoon, while Nino was bent over his task in the vineyards, a pair of fine leather boots came into his peripheral vision. The man wearing them stopped to hover over him, but Nino kept working. He could guess the boots' owner even before the man ordered him to his feet. Nino rose, but refused to face his father.

"Look at me," Nicola bellowed. But Nino would not move.

"Don't you know who I am?" Nicola demanded. Still, Nino stared at his own sandaled feet and refused to reply.

"*Rispetto!*" Nicola shouted. "Look at me. I am your father and I demand you respect me."

Gripping his grafting knife tighter, Nino raised his face to glare into his father's. "I have no respect for you." Without another word, he turned and walked away.

By the time he was nineteen, Nino could no longer abide working for his father. He grew more somber and quiet than usual as he grappled with the agonizing alternative—to go with his uncle to Detroit and support his mother and Angelina from there. Nino swore to his mother that she would not lose another son. He'd return to her just as soon as he could build up savings enough for them to get by. His passport said he was going to America for three years.

In 1909 there was no crying need for grafters in Detroit, so Nino started out paving roads and sidewalks for a dollar and twenty-five cents a day, the same amount the Sicilian couple charged him monthly for the room they rented him. The remainder of his wages went toward reimbursing his uncle for the boat ticket, for the meager meals he cooked for himself, and to his mother in Sicily.

After a year, Nino sought work that paid better. A friend at the boardinghouse, who worked as a bricklayer, offered to introduce him to his boss. The boss sized up the young man—he was five feet five inches tall and slight—and told him he wasn't hiring. Nino nodded, but he didn't leave. He had no other job prospects to investigate that day, so he decided to stick around and watch his friend work. He came back the following morning, and then the day after that, watching and studying the technique of neatly sandwiching cement between bricks. On the fourth day, the boss again told Nino that he wasn't hiring. On the fifth day, Nino picked up a trowel, fell in beside his friend, and began laying brick. The boss watched Nino that morning with practiced indifference on his face. The young Italian's work was neater and faster than that of men who'd spent years in the building trades. Without a word, the boss watched again on the sixth day and the seventh, as the young man put in more than an honest day's work for nothing but the experience. The next morning, when Nino again silently set to work beside his friend, the boss walked over and told Nino what an impression he had made with both his work and his moxie. With a handshake, he told Nino he was putting him on the payroll, retroactive to the first day.

Nino relished working outdoors and took pride in his skill with the trowel. He was growing buildings instead of trees, but best of all, he was sending a monthly sum of money home to his mother and Angelina, tucked inside letters he dictated to a friend and then signed with an X.

Detroit was nothing like Mazara, in whose port teeming with fishermen and fishmongers Nino had learned to swim. Whenever he got homesick for the sea, Nino walked down to the Detroit River to watch the boats pass between him and the lights twinkling in Canada, which sat a mile away on the opposite shore. Sometimes before work he would head to nearby Eastern Market, congested with open air stalls heaped with the crisp produce the farmers had picked before the last rays of moonlight slipped from the sky. Sicilian was the language there, and the market's narrow aisles, its color, fragrance, and the chorus of haggling voices reminded him of the bustling fish market adjacent to Mazara's port, where the fishmongers hawked each day's catch and gutted the customers' dinner while it still quivered.

Often Nino would make his way to Belle Isle, the island park that sat at the end of a wooden bridge in the middle of the Detroit River. Crisscrossed with canals and trails running through its woods, the two-and-a-half-mile-long island was the only place where Detroiters could access the river for swimming. On scorching summer afternoons, they could ride the Belle Isle ferry up and down the river the entire day for a nickel. On scorching summer nights when sleep eluded them, they would flock to Belle Isle's bathhouse, cool off with a swim, and then spread their blankets to sleep under the stars.

Nino lived frugally, spending little on himself so that he could send his mother a few extra dollars at holidays and still be able to stash away a "kitty" to take back with him to Mazara. What he couldn't afford, he didn't buy. Italians in America were proud of living within their means, and being in debt was frowned upon. It was enough that debt had been their lot in Sicily.

As houses and stores multiplied under the sweep of Nino's

trowel, one year turned to two, two to three, and his uncle returned to Mazara alone. Nino had too small a "kitty" saved. Three
years turned to four, and the sound of his mother's and Angelina's
voices dimmed more in Nino's head and twinged much harder in
his heart.

A neighbor who knew how desperately Nino missed his family repeatedly offered him moonlighting jobs. Jobs that paid well. The
neighbor belonged to a group of men from Mazara who took certain community matters into their own hands, just as they had
in Sicily. There were Corleonese groups, Palermitani groups,
Mazarese groups, Terrasinese groups, groups from every large or
little *comune* in Sicily, and all of them were vying for turf in
America. Nino was polite enough, friendly enough even, with his
Mazarese neighbor, but he was also proud of his life of hard honest work. Year after year, he declined his neighbor's offer of a second job.

Five years had come and gone without a return home when
Nino heard through the grapevine that a family, recently arrived
from Palermo, had just moved into the neighborhood. A family
with a good-looking marriageable daughter. It was the sort of
news that made the young men of the community extremely interested in attending Sunday Mass.

Chapter Five ❧

My great-grandmother Concetta Lupica.

Corleone, Sicily, 1903

While her brothers and sister slept upstairs in the small cramped loft of the stone house, Francesca spent the nights of her infancy downstairs in her parents' bedroom. It was not a proper room per se, but an alcove partitioned off with a curtain from the one large room that made up the basic Sicilian house, serving as its kitchen, dining room, donkey stable, chicken coop, and bathroom. Francesca slept on a soft pillow tucked into a basket that sat on the floor alongside Concetta's side of the high bed typical of Sicilian households, right beside the step stool her mother needed to climb onto the bed. When Francesca cried in the night, Concetta would raise the baby to the bed top by pulling on the long strings attached to the basket. Concetta would nurse her, swaddle her tightly, tuck her striped blankets again snugly, and then lower her back to the floor until she whimpered again.

In the daytime she stayed by Concetta's side, watching from her basket as her mother's feet swung over the side of the high mattress in search of the step stool, signaling the start of a new day. Before dawn lit the sky, Domenico—when he was at home—stepped down from the stool on his side of the bed, to get ready for work. Once dressed, he'd head to the kitchen to take up the knapsack Concetta had packed the night before with a chunk of bread and something else to sustain him during the workday; usually it was an onion or a tomato or a piece of fruit.

Concetta's day always began before full dawn. After dressing, she would shoo the chickens from the kitchen, lead the donkey out of the house from his "stable" behind the front, and only, door, where she'd hitched him the night before, and then sweep the animal dung out the door. Like all the *contadini*, each night the Costas brought their animals inside to sleep, and each morning they sent them out again into the fresh air. Unlike the more wealthy among the peasants, however, the Costas had no pig, which would have spent the night nestled beneath the open kitchen hearth where Concetta cooked the family meals.

By the time Concetta moved aside the chairs—rough-hewn, with rope seats woven from agave—and swept the kitchen's hard-packed chalk and mud floor, she would hear the chatter of female voices beginning to rise outside neighboring doors, ending the solitude of the night. Concetta would join these other women in a procession to an outer section of town where they would dump out the lid-covered white pots each family kept in a far corner of the kitchen. Before breakfast, and then again late in the afternoon, the women had to take care of the family toilet. It was an odious task, one the Sicilians likened to the ignominy Jesus endured, sarcastically calling the foul chore "making the way of the cross."

Upon her return from the sewage ditch, Concetta would climb the rickety ladder leading to the loft and rouse the four older children from their beds. After she dressed them and led them outside to brush the sleep from their hair under the pergola laced with grapevines, she set to preparing their meager morning meal, carefully cutting small chunks off the last loaf of bread. The rest of that bread had to last them until Saturday, when she would bake two fresh loaves for the week ahead.

At least once a week, she would knock the dust from the open wooden cabinet that held their colorful pottery dishes and bowls, and from the chest of drawers on which various knickknacks sat alongside the baby Jesus, entwined with flowers and ribbons. Once a year she would take down the pictures of the saints who peered at them from every wall, so that Domenico and the older boys could whitewash the entire house and erase the year's worth of soot produced by their brazier.

If Domenico bemoaned Francesca's arrival, Concetta must have been thrilled, finally, to have a second daughter. The boys might help their father earn the family's bread, but they were useless around the house. Their birthright not only excused them from "women's work," but made certain that they increased it.

Concetta no doubt suckled her longed-for daughters impatiently. Weary from nonstop pregnancies while juggling the demands of a household and animals and the sole care of five toddlers whose father was continually away either working or dancing his way through the Sicilian countryside, she was anxious for the day when she could put to use those four extra hands that God had given just to her.

Born last to a large peasant family in Partinico, Concetta Lupica was no stranger to hard work. She was already long-faced and stoop-shouldered in even her earliest photographs. As a child, she lived in the crowded hovel that her family had to share with other destitute peasants also eking out their existence on a sugar-cane farm.

One scorching harvest afternoon while the men were in the fields hacking down canes, the *gabellotto* strode out to the field, gun on his hip, and cornered her father. "Tell me, Pasquale, perhaps you've been taking some of this sugarcane? You know, to earn a few cents?" Pasquale swiped the sweat from his eyes and denied the theft with an oath, asking if the *gabellotto* truly took him for that much of a fool. Still, the overseer kept his eye on Pasquale and before long confronted him again.

"So, Pasquale. You think that what falls to the ground is yours? That you can just take it for yourself and sneak off to make some extra money? Well, you just take your family from my farm and never set your foot in this place again."

In that instant, the Lupicas had no home, no money, and no prospects for earning their next meal. Desperate, Pasquale threw his hungry family on the mercy of relatives while he searched for work. For a time he peddled vegetables for a farmer, and Concetta spent each growing season seated beside her father in their wooden cart. At six, seven, and eight years of age, she spent her childhood jumping down from the cart with a little sack for the housewife and running back to her papa with the few coins in payment tied inside her little handkerchief.

Winters when Pasquale could find no work, they lived from hand to mouth. There were numerous nights during her childhood that Concetta went to bed hungry.

. . .

In the days after Francesca's birth, Concetta passed the time sitting out in the October sunshine with her children, as did all the other mothers and children on the narrow cobblestone street lined with squat stone houses. The Costa youngsters ate slowly and carefully, leaving no crumbs to share with the chickens, underfoot and eager to peck up any spills. In another week the welcome fall rains would come to drench the parched earth and cool down the fiery summer air. Concetta nibbled at her crust while Francesca nibbled at her breast, and she tried to push from her mind the familiar niggling worries about who might be sharing her breakfast with Domenico this morning. She'd pretended not to hear the snide whispers of the neighbor women. *Caccia gaddina,* they called her husband—a hen chaser.

She took small comfort from the old Sicilian saying her mother often reminded her of: "Kiss, kiss, honeypot, but you are the *puttana* and I am the wife."

Like that of all Sicilian women, even to this day, Concetta's surname did not change when she married Domenico Costa. While modern Western women might herald this ancient custom of Italian females retaining their own names as forward-thinking and empowering, the practice bears no correlation to the feminist reclamation of identity begun in the 1960s. Upon her engagement to Domenico, Concetta relinquished absolutely any sense of self. Passed from father to fiancé, she was Domenico's now, and upon their marriage she would have do his bidding, share his plate, his bed, and often his affections. In her husband's eyes, she would forever come after their children, who themselves, until they were old enough to work in the fields or in the house, came after the family's animals.

Concetta's was an arranged marriage, as all in Sicily were at that time. But unlike nearly every other young *fidanzata,* who met her *fidanzato* for the first time when they stood before the priest, at least Concetta knew in advance the man her mother had chosen to dominate her for the rest of her life. The trouble was, her older sister knew her fiancé, too.

If young Francesca Costa was the most beautiful of her siblings, her mother was not. Concetta was considered among the least lovely of the sisters in her own family. Her older sister, Rosalia, whose scowl was overhung with a big black moustache, was the only one who looked more *brutta*. Concetta might be considered handsome by today's standards, with pleasant features arranged symmetrically in a long, oval face. She had a high forehead, slender nose, a wide full mouth, and sorrowful blue eyes, a genetic gift of the Normans. Yet it was not lost on anyone that her husband was much better looking than Concetta was, even on her wedding day. It was a fact that Domenico was always ready to point out.

Peasant girls like Concetta did not grow up dreaming of their wedding day, romanticizing the event the way American girls do. Among the Sicilian *contadini*, the groom routinely struck his bride in front of their guests, either at the wedding feast or as she first stepped over the threshold into her new home. She accepted the traditional blow, just as she accepted that marriage would simply take her from a life of servitude in her father's home to one of the same in her husband's. A bride's situation was worse, in fact, for it was frowned upon for a Sicilian father to regularly beat a daughter. Not so a husband.

When Concetta married Domenico, he most likely would have paired his public smack with either a speech of his own composition or, as was more usual, the words of a Sicilian proverb—"A woman is like a cat. Pet her and she'll claw you." At her birth, a female's suffering was acknowledged, but at her marriage, it was put on public display.

Concetta and Domenico were engaged for more than a year, their wedding postponed while her widowed mother struggled to assemble her dowry of linens, clothing, and a pair of gold earrings.

Proper furniture was nowhere to be had in Partinico, so Concetta's mother announced that a shopping expedition to Palermo was necessary to obtain a mattress for the *fidanzati,* the engaged couple. Francesca di Giovanni packed some food for the trip and set out for Palermo with her daughter and Domenico in tow. Since they had been able to scrape together only enough money to rent one hotel room for one night, Francesca also took along Rosalia to serve as chaperone.

No match had yet been struck for twenty-one-year-old Rosalia, and when Francesca allowed Concetta to marry rather than pair off her female offspring in proper order, it must have exacerbated the humiliation of her less attractive daughter. Rosalia surely had mixed feelings on that trip—pity for herself, anger at her mother, jealousy of her younger sister—all jumbled together with the excitement and adventure of seeing the big seaport city with its grand Royal Palace, Norman churches, teeming Byzantine street markets, medieval ghettos, labyrinthine streets, and bustling port.

To Palermo they went, procuring for the *fidanzati* a marriage bed in an affordable price range. The shopping and sightseeing completed, the four travelers returned to the hotel, where everyone slept together in the one small room, dressed from neck to ankle in the same dusty clothing they'd worn on their journey.

Several weeks after they had returned from securing the marriage mattress for Concetta and Domenico, Rosalia came to her mother with a question.

"Is it possible to get pregnant if you've slept with a man just one time?"

Horrified, Francesca repeatedly slapped the deflowered chaperone, raining curses on her head with every blow. Then Francesca di Giovanni ran to shove into a satchel the sheets and linens and nightgowns they'd been accumulating in Concetta's *casa de noce,* the brightly painted hope chest that would sit at the foot of her marriage bed. She glanced up at the cross that hung above the bed with a loop of palm fronds tucked behind it, and offered up a hasty prayer. If her male relatives got wind of the news that Domenico had ruined Rosalia, it was those two who would be married before the week was out. Hurrying, Francesca gathered up whatever else she could spare to add to the bundle. Breathless, she cornered Concetta and pressed the haphazard trousseau into her daughter's arms.

"You must go. Run away with Domenico, now! Elope! We can't wait to finish your *corredo*. There is no time. Go, *subito*! Do as I say quickly, before your sister steals away for good your *fidanzato*."

Without even a horrified glance at her weeping sister, Concetta ran from the square stone house. Her heart and her head were pounding from this craziness—she should elope? *Fuitina* was usually the solution for young women promised to men they did not love, a Sicilian loophole through which a desperate couple could defy their elders to tie the knot. What had her beast of a sister done to her? Despite Domenico's betrayal, she blamed Rosalia more. Like other Sicilian women, she understood that his was male behavior that she'd have to accept.

She and Domenico rode his donkey to a neighboring town, where the priest married them that same day. Domenico needn't have slapped Concetta's face on their wedding day. Her sister already had.

There was no party for the newlyweds upon their return. Concetta came home a married woman pregnant with a child she would soon miscarry.

Though Rosalia's errant period finally arrived, Concetta adamantly refused to speak to her or to acknowledge her existence, despite their mother's efforts toward reconciliation. Concetta's hatred of Rosalia was so intense, she could not even bring herself to look at her ugly older sister.

Chapter Six ❧

Appearances were of the utmost importance in the Costa family, as in most Sicilian families. Sicilians commanded their children to behave without questioning, required that dowries meet a certain minimum, and demanded that their women remain chaste, living by a social code that was enforced by the watchful eyes of their relatives and neighbors. Even among close family members, Sicilian tongues sat ready to cluck over the slightest impropriety or whiff of laxity. When a family owned little but their honor, that honor became everything.

It was a warm fall afternoon in 1914 when Concetta thrust a broom into Giuseppina's hands with orders to tidy up such appearances. "Just look at all those leaves piled across the porch. Do you want the neighbors to think we are *sporco* [dirty]? Go outside and get busy," she ordered. Even just onto the porch, however, there was no chance she'd allow her eldest daughter outside alone. She sent Francesca outside after her, to chaperone.

It was while thirteen-year-old Giuseppina swept the porch that afternoon that Antonino Mazzarino walked down the street and into her heart. It was his curly hair that got her, she told me, so dark and unruly. He wore it parted on the side, and it was so thick and kinky it mushroomed from his scalp like a lopsided Afro. Nino's pace seemed to slow a step as he passed, and Giuseppina's heartbeat accelerated. He was the most handsome man she had ever seen. The gorgeous creature with the curly hair was all she and Francesca could swoon about for days.

Nino fell for Giuseppina the second he spotted her, and he wasn't inside the door of his boardinghouse before he was bombarding his landlady with a dozen questions about the small dark-haired beauty on Monroe Street and about her family. The Italian community in Detroit was large, but not so large that the grapevine could not gather information quickly. He asked at the grocer's, he inquired of neighbors and his friends, hungry for information about the girl he'd seen on the porch.

At the time he brought his family to join him in Detroit, Domenic was already known in the Sicilian community as a *consigliere,* an adviser or mediator whose word settled disputes. Within days, Nino learned that Giuseppina Costa was the same *consigliere*'s daughter he'd heard had recently arrived from Sicily, and that she was a virtuous girl.

It took another week before the shy young bricklayer could work up enough courage to climb the stairs to that front porch to ask her father for permission to call on her.

"You and me, we talk first, signore," Domenic informed Nino, ushering him into the living room.

Had the two young people still been in Sicily, it would have been their mothers who made the marriage inquiries and the ultimate decisions for the two families, and Nino and Giuseppina would have had no say in the matter. Nino's mother would have asked Concetta if perhaps she had a hen for sale that was about fourteen years of age, and since Giuseppina was quite agreeable to the match, Concetta would have replied in the affirmative rather than gently rebuff her with the sincere regret that the hen she had for sale was just nine years old.

Eavesdropping from the upstairs hallway, Giuseppina and Francesca were barely able to contain their excitement as Nino began to speak. He told their father how his father—a duke, the people called him because of the vineyards he owned in Mazara— had become smitten with another woman when Nino was still a toddler. How the duke had simply turned his back on Giovannina and their three children, abandoning them to a life of poverty while he married his new love in a civil ceremony and quickly got started fathering a second family, promising a church wedding once Giovannina died.

Nino recounted how his mother had taken to weaving cane into backs and seats for wooden chairs to support her children. How, at age three, he'd run to scoop up cow and horse droppings that his mother clandestinely sold for pennies, for since Italy had been unified, what fell in the streets or grew over into public areas no longer belonged to the peasants, only to the municipality.

At five, he began to work for a blacksmith. At seven, he helped his brother herd sheep. There had been no time for school, and no money for it either, so he had never learned to read or write. He signed his name to official documents with a bold X, he told Domenic matter-of-factly. Street signs were superfluous to him. He made his way about Detroit by quickly memorizing landmarks.

Upstairs, Giuseppina was already crazy in love. Aside from the fact that the young man sounded polite and respectful, how could her father not be impressed with his initiative and resolve? Her hopes were buoyed when the formal conversation came to an end, and the sisters listened as their father ushered Nino to the door.

"As you know, I will make some inquiries. And if I like what I hear, and if the *christiani*"—a word Sicilians use for "people"— "say, 'Antonino Mazzarino, he's a good man,' then we'll see."

As the front door closed behind Nino, Giuseppina and Francesca darted to the upstairs window to catch a glimpse of him as he headed down the street.

The Costa boys were used to hard manual labor, but although Henry Ford encouraged his employees to learn English, they were not used to studying. Still, in the fall of 1914, they decided to take their boss's offer seriously. As repercussions of the war in Europe reached Detroit, mills shut down and eighty thousand newly jobless men roamed the city's streets. Citizens donated sacks of food to help feed them, while the Detroit Board of Commerce recruited doctors and pharmacies to donate medical care and medicine for their sick children and wives. Although the Board of Commerce strove to find them new jobs, they succeeded in putting only twenty thousand men back to work. The other sixty thousand went unemployed and starving due to their inability to communicate in English.

With the depression of the winter of 1914–15 came the push to teach Detroit's immigrants the language. When Henry Ford discovered that five thousand of his thirteen thousand employees could not speak English, he opened the Ford English School. Other employers came through, tacking posters to the school's bulletin boards, urging that with schooling, immigrants could "become better citizens and get better jobs." Factories slipped notices in pay envelopes, offering raises and job security incentives to those who became fluent in English. There wasn't a place the Italians, Russians, Greeks, Belgians, Romanians, Armenians, and Poles could go to escape the message. Sales clerks who determined they were waiting on immigrants packaged night school advertisements in with their purchases. Saloon keepers plastered their walls with posters—"Learn English and Get Better Pay." Clergymen preached it from the pulpits, editors of Detroit's foreign language newspapers harped on it from their editorial pages. The message took root. By the following fall, the Costa boys were already reading on a first-grade level and the Board of Education had to turn away applicants for night school.

Although the feelers Domenic put out in the community about Giuseppina's twenty-three-year-old prospective suitor garnered only glowing reports, he nevertheless decided he would "watch" Nino Mazzarino for several months before sending word that he'd given consent for the courtship to begin.

Domenic told Nino he was allowed to call on Giuseppina only when he and his wife were both at home. He was welcome, even expected, to join them for Sunday dinner. Nino and Giuseppina both knew that physical contact, even a handshake, between them was verboten. Concetta or Domenic would open the front door to welcome him, but never Giuseppina. She could not even offer to bring him a cup of coffee or a glass of water. Even that much contact between unmarried men and women was highly improper, so her mother always saw to the serving of any refreshments.

At dinner, Nino was required to sit at one end of the table near Giuseppina's father or brothers. In the living room, he sat on the horsehair couch at one end of the room while Giuseppina sat on a chair at the other, with Domenic and Concetta plopped on stiff seats in the center of the room from which to supervise. Concetta only excused herself to stir the spaghetti sauce or when baby Michael needed his diaper changed. Across the doily-covered furniture and her parents' heads, Giuseppina chatted with her curly-haired suitor while her parents sat silent as the walls and pretended not to listen.

Often Francesca, Agata, Maria, Luigi, and Salvatore darted in and out, wide-eyed and giggling, always curious about the young man with such an interest in their eldest sister. Nino sat mesmerized by Giuseppina's full mouth and dark eyes and her wry humor. He didn't even blink the first time her smile broadened to a grin and exposed the gap where her two permanently missing top teeth should have been.

In Sicily, their courtship and engagement would have lasted anywhere from three to five years. Sicilians adhered to a proverb that prescribed eighteen as the perfect age for a woman to marry, and twenty-eight for a man. By that age, the young man would have saved enough money to buy a house if his parents had not been able to provide one for the newlyweds, as the majority of Sicilian families did. He would also use the time to earn the money for most of the furnishings for the new house, for a good black dress for his bride, bolts of cloth for her to make other dresses, and for the earrings and shawl and other gifts he would give to her as their wedding neared.

. . .

Six months of these Sunday visits passed before Domenic consented to allow Nino and Josie—she now insisted on being called by an Americanized version of her name—some time to visit by themselves in the living room, provided one of her parents was at home and within earshot. Still, there was no physical contact between the young couple. They continued to sit, she on one side of the room, he on the opposite. The following spring Josie turned fourteen, and finally Domenic gave Nino permission to propose marriage. The engagement—the *conuscenza*—as in Sicily, would last a year. The wedding would take place in Detroit in the winter of 1916.

Immediately, Nino dictated a letter to his mother, asking her to purchase the engagement ring in Sicily with the money he'd enclosed because he'd found nothing in Detroit that could compare with the delicate filigree of the Italian settings he'd seen in Palermo or that gleamed with the same deep luster of the Italian 18-karat gold.

By then, Nino was finally able to set aside some of his paycheck for his own future. With the recent marriage of his sister, Angelina, her new husband was not only supporting his wife but helping with their mother's care.

Unlike their future brother-in-law, Josie's older brothers spent every dime they made on themselves and contributed nothing to the family income, even though they knew their father played bocce every Sunday, hoping he'd win two or three dollars to help feed them. Domenic couldn't change their behavior, and he couldn't throw them out of his house without raising eyebrows in the community. By day, they grew muscular wrestling the crankcases and axles that came rolling toward them on the assembly line. Then they blew their paychecks buying stylish suits, shirts, shoes, and hats. At night they spiffed themselves up in fifteen-dollar three-piece suits to carouse in the streets, drinking, gambling, hustling, and procuring the services of women, sometimes several in the course of an evening. They saw the inside of the house only to eat, to sleep, or to toss their fancy duds down the laundry chute and demand that their sisters wash and iron them—perfectly.

The girls sweated over the ribbed metal washboard in the basement, using yellow soap to scrub the railroad soot from their father's work clothes and the dark grease ground into their brothers'. Francesca was certain some of this thick grease must be lodged in her brothers' ears, since they now bellowed from the moment they came in the door, all the way through dinner. The boys hollered that they couldn't hear themselves over the din of the auto plant factory still ringing in their ears.

Mr. Ford's promise of five dollars a day had strings attached, the Costas soon discovered. In addition to an honest day's work, he expected morality and good living standards among his employees. Furthermore, across the nation, alcohol consumption was swiftly going out of favor. By 1913, one county at a time, temperance advocates had convinced enough voters to enact dry laws to make booze illegal for half the citizens of the country.

In Detroit, spirits still flowed, even though forty of Michigan's eighty-three counties were already dry by 1911. Detroit's Italians, like other European immigrants, swallowed wine, grappa, or beer with their meals more often than they did water. Echoes of their days of indentured servitude in the old country reverberated through the Italian workers' homes when investigators from Mr. Ford's "Sociological Department" showed up unannounced to check their iceboxes for beer or wine and their homes for cleanliness. Domenic bristled that in America his employer could dictate how he ran his home.

Though all the nightlife they could handle sat under the gaudily lit marquees of the large theater district on Monroe Street, just a few short blocks from their house, and they could either walk or ride the streetcar anywhere they wanted to go, for some of their nighttime activities the Costa boys needed a car. Their father wasn't a *consigliere* for nothing. With his catbird seat on what was going on in the streets, he made sure always to slip in a recommendation for his sons. *Perhaps you could use some extra muscle stealing tires? Say the word if you want somebody taught a lesson.* His sons were as good as any one of his *cumparis'* kids who were doing this work. No reason they shouldn't find a way to a piece of the action.

The action he found them helped his older sons buy a car long before their father could afford one. They spent days circling the models, checking out every auto in the sixteen dealerships along Jefferson's Automobile Row before deciding to pool their money to buy the $360 low-end Ford. Now, the brothers could go out on "jobs," each taking his turn behind the wheel while the other two served as lookouts.

As they'd expected, Nino had turned them down when they'd asked their future brother-in-law to go in on the purchase. He'd keep walking wherever he needed to go, and had no interest in helping them steal tires or transport prostitutes—escort service, the Costa boys called it—even if they procured him a driver's license. He told them he had a neighbor high up in one of the Mafiosi gangs who made similar overtures from time to time, but that he had no desire to get himself mixed up in any of these doings.

He wasn't a flashy dresser like they were, he didn't own a gun, and his gambling habits were limited to the occasional loud and friendly game of *morra*. Now that he was nearly their brother-in-law, Rocco, Pasquale, and Angelo hounded Nino to accompany them to the brothels. Sicilians encouraged engaged men to consort with prostitutes to slake the sexual hunger they believed intensified as the wedding day neared. But no matter how many times they cajoled him, no matter how many times they called him a sissy, Nino refused.

The brothers were derisive about the young bricklayer's refusal to perfect his prowess, curious about his reluctance to make a fast buck, but while they rolled their eyes and commented behind his back about how foolish it was to pass up such sure money, they also admitted they knew a good man when they saw one. Nino's lifelong resolve to earn his money slowly and honestly, my grandmother told me, earned him the authentic respect of his brothers-in-law.

As she had in Sicily, Concetta lay awake at night worrying about her sons. She knew that when Domenic left after dinner it was to play a game of *scopa* with his cronies, visit another woman, or mediate a dispute, but she believed her boys were up to more. All the young Italian boys in Detroit ran in gangs with others from their hometowns. She listened to talk about the young men's doings out on the street—how this one had gotten arrested, how another one had been deported back to Italy. When she overheard Domenic talking up their sons to the men he counseled, her blood ran cold. Although she couldn't read the papers, she knew of the latest headlines about feuds and fights among the young Sicilians. Even after her boys stumbled up the stairs smelling of booze and perfume, she lay in the dark listening to their snores and she worried and she prayed. She made excuses when the girls found blood on their brothers' shirts, and the boys made excuses when it was scabbed and ugly across their cheeks or knuckles. While she begged Him to keep her sons alive, Concetta thanked God that her Josie's Nino wanted no part of that street life. Only God knew what her sons were getting mixed up in out there.

Chapter Seven ❧

Corleone, October 1903

To the whoops of his children, my great-grandfather Domenico arrived home from his travels with a pocket full of money. Enough winnings to buy food for La Festa dei Morti, All Souls' Day, on November 2, and to purchase each of the children a small toy. All Sicilian children anticipated finding sweets on that morning, sneaked into the house by their dead ancestors sometime during the night between Tutti Santi—All Saints' Day—and All Souls' Day. Luckier children might also find a tiny present, often the only one they'd receive the entire year. This year, Domenico's children would not go disappointed.

In the less than three weeks since she'd given birth to Francesca, Concetta's days had found a rhythm and her husband was back to help sow the wheat fields. It was a race to get every seed into the ground while the fall rains fell, and each year the *contadini* who worked the farms simply crossed themselves and otherwise ignored All Saints' Day and All Souls' Day, working straight through the holy days of prayer and rest that marked the beginning of November. For the past two weeks, the *contadini* had toiled from early morning until sunset, ploughing the earth to ready it for the planting season. The sowing would consume every day until December.

With Francesca on her hip, Concetta stirred her pots, timing dinner for Domenico's return from the fields. He hung up his cap, took out his handkerchief, and, as always, wiped off his chair before he sat down. His family gathered around the long wooden table and waited for him to bless the bread with the sign of the cross before cutting off a small slice for each of them, after giving himself the first piece. Even the youngest Sicilian child knew that Papa cut the bread at the table, that no one ever set a loaf upside down, and that everyone had to kiss their bread before taking a single bite. As Domenico and Concetta sat eating from the same bowl of *minestra*, a thin vegetable soup, he informed her that he and his brother, Mario, had decided that in two days their two families were returning to Partinico for the *festa*.

They had no dead ancestors buried in Corleone. How could they have a proper cemetery picnic celebration to honor their dead if all their dead were in the ground a day's ride north? Besides, the little ones were already worrying about their candied presents, asking how their dead great-grandparents would know their way to the new house in Corleone.

The children looked up from their soup bowls, already tingling with anticipation. "Are you *pazzo*?" Concetta cried out. "We leave now, you lose your job. Then we'll eat boiled water without any vegetables."

"Don't you call me crazy, woman," he grunted, gesturing with a chunk of bread. "It's decided. The fields will still be here when we get back."

Domenico informed her that he and his brother had each arranged to borrow a cart and a second donkey to hitch alongside their own. He would take care of selecting the children's presents. She had two days to prepare the special holiday cookies and sweets, the food for the journey, and the food for the *festa* at the cemetery.

Domenico was still snoring on the following two mornings when Concetta dragged herself from their bed even earlier than usual to nurse Francesca and remove the large wooden board from the wall to begin the day's baking. Several kinds of cookies were expected to be made, including those eaten only once a year, marked with a skull and crossbones. Another, flavored with anise seed, she remembered her *nonna* had always enjoyed, and she would bake some of those, too, to set out on Nonna's grave, for the dead were invited to partake of the *festa*, too.

On the Saturday when they were to leave, Domenico was still soundly sleeping when Concetta rose in the dead of night to bake the week's two loaves of bread. Before setting out her ingredients, she uttered the prayer that always began the bread baking: "In the name of the Father, the Son, and the Holy Spirit. Saint Agata, fire up the oven plates. Now my work is done, do yours, Virgin Mary." As she measured flour onto the wooden board, she heard the neighborhood men leave for the fields and her stomach clenched with another quick prayer—that Domenico and Mario would still have jobs three days from now.

Concetta worked the dough quickly in the *sbriga*, a wooden trough with a long handle for kneading. She still had a full morning's work ahead, even though she had already organized most of the *festa* picnic delicacies the day before, packing the several varieties of cookies along with some dried fruit and a special treat to share with their dead relatives—the nice hunk of fresh *touma* cheese that Domenico's dancing had bought for the *festa*.

When the dough had risen and was ready to fashion into loaves, Concetta again turned to heaven with the customary prayer that her bread would bake to perfection. "Bread grow, as God blessed you! Grow, bread, in the oven as God grew in the world! Saint Francis, fresh bread! Saint Cataldo, fragrant bread! Saint Zita, fine of crust and crumb! Saint Nicholas, let it grow as big as a mill!"

She slipped the loaves into the open hearth to bake and did what every mother taught her daughter to do—shook out the towel on which the dough had risen before she put it back in the table's drawer. If she forgot to shake out the bread's "bed," she knew her loaves would emerge from the *forno* flat as a blade of grass and hard as a rock.

While she waited for the bread to turn golden, Concetta turned to preparing the frittatas, a special addition to the basket of food they would take with them to the family plot. Unless it was a *festa* or a special Sunday or one of them was very ill, Domenico never let her take any of their chickens' eggs for the family. They were too valuable not to sell.

She selected several large eggs he had given her permission to use and beat them together with the crumbs she'd carefully swept from the table and saved in a little bowl each time she'd cut bread for Domenico's lunch over the past week. She took the crust she'd hoarded from last week's bread, dried now, and grated it into the bowl, careful not to let a single crumb drop to the floor. She didn't want to spend eternity gathering up bread crumbs from God's floor with her eyelashes, as another superstition went. Then she tossed in a small handful of grated Parmesan cheese and some freshly chopped basil picked from the small patch of herbs near the house. She spooned the mixture, thick as pancake batter, into the skillet sizzling with hot olive oil. There was one frittata for each of them, and two for Domenico.

The smell of the frying patties wafted up into the loft, rousing the Costa children from their cot. They came paddling down the ladder in their patched nightshirts, hungry and chattering with anticipation of the celebration and the presents they'd find in Partinico. "Can we have some now?" they begged, while Concetta shooed them away from the frying pan, telling them that these were for the *festa*. After she'd wrapped the hot frittatas in a towel, Concetta cleaned up the children and dressed them. She'd already packed a pillowcase with their finest clothes, which she'd dress them in for the cemetery outing on Monday.

While Domenico led the donkeys away to water them in the nearby piazza's fountain, Concetta quickly tidied up herself. Her last chore was to rip numerous strips from an old piece of toweling.

She packed most of these in the pillowcase with their clothing and then secured a thick wad of them between her legs to catch the blood still seeping from her contracting uterus.

Finally, all was ready. Calling good-byes to the women and old men seated outside their homes who wished them a happy *festa* in return, the Costas made their way down a maze of narrow streets to the donkeys waiting with the borrowed carts. Domenico slapped his woven palm leaf hat on his head and smiled. He nearly danced around the cart's two large wheels as he swung his children up and settled them in between the packages of food and clothing. The *festa* was his reprieve from work and he planned to dance and eat and enjoy his holiday.

Bone weary, Concetta hoisted herself into the wagon and put Francesca to her breast. As Domenico flicked his switch at the donkey, she hoped for two things: that the fall rains had not washed out any of the road between here and Partinico, and that she wouldn't bleed through her skirts before they managed to stop later in the afternoon to relieve themselves by the side of the road.

As the cart lurched forward, Francesca began to choke on her mother's milk. The baby's choking turned to sobs that would not abate, and Domenico gestured at his wife with the switch.

"Foolish woman, shut up that child."

Her right hand fisted beneath Francesca's pillow, its knuckles pointed toward Domenico. She'd lived enough years with his quixotic temper and did not doubt that he would lash her, even while she held a baby at her breast. Lips clenched, she seethed with every curse she could not utter and imagined every blow she wished she could inflict on him. Though her culture demanded that a husband be persistent and a wife patient, stoicism did not sit well with her. Rebellion coursed through her mind, her veins, and even into the milk with which she nursed Francesca. Given the chance, she had no doubt she could match her husband's brutality.

L'America, she thought. Her *cummari*'s husband had gone to America to find work, and five years later he had sent money for the steamship tickets for his wife and children. Life was better there, she knew. Everything was different there; people had jobs, food.

Concetta was powerless to alter her lot with Domenico, for every wife in Sicily had to be kept in her place, and that place was subordinate to her husband. The proverbs she'd heard since childhood had taught her all she could expect from marriage, and Domenico, like his father before him, subscribed to every one: A wife should be treated firmly. Like a good weapon, she should be cared for properly. Like a hat, she should be kept straight. And like a mule, she should be given plenty of work and occasional beatings.

Concetta transferred Francesca to her other breast, readjusting her shawl to conceal the nursing baby. Maybe her daughters would find their way to l'America and a life different from her own.

Chapter Eight ❧

Partinico, like all of Sicily's towns and cities, still resonates with
the echoes of cultures past. While its name probably springs
from the Latin Parthenicum, its origins are almost certainly
Greek. Muslims called it Bartniq in the Middle Ages, a time when
this mountaintop village produced lush, abundant crops of cotton
and of henna, a plant used to make dyes.

Concetta Lupica had little inkling of the history layered on the
landscapes she surveyed as the wooden donkey cart jostled the
young family down one craggy mountainside and up another. My
great-grandmother couldn't read, she couldn't write, and she had
no idea that five hundred years earlier there had been mighty
forests surrounding her birthplace or that Partinico had been
made fertile with sugarcane and grape arbors. She had no clue
that her destitute hometown was once crowned with the grand
country homes of Palermo's nobility. In her generation, it was rare
enough that the male children of the *contadini* spent even a single
day in school. For daughters, it was unheard of. Nearly everything
Concetta learned was experiential. She grew up, like my great-
great-grandparents before her, under the dual yoke of poverty and
political impotence, ignorant of the history that had forged their
destiny.

The balmy breezes of a European Indian summer caressed the
small entourage as they made their way downhill from Corleone.
Concetta hummed folk lullabies to the sleeping infant, cradling

Francesca with one arm and keeping the other hand free to swat at the four fidgety little ones piled among the packages behind her. The first leg of their journey took them within sight of the marvelous La Ficuzza, the last natural forest remaining in Sicily. Every other timberland on the island had been leveled centuries before by the Romans, who felled the trees to transform them into seaworthy vessels for their vast fleets. They cleared the land to pave the way for boundless fields of hardy durum wheat, forcing the Sicilian peasants to labor in the breadbasket of their empire while condemning their island homeland to a perpetual battle with erosion.

Concetta pointed in the direction of the grand forest and regaled her little ones with stories about the woodland's countless baby animals and colorful birds, many of them creatures they could imagine only from their mama's descriptions. She entranced them with tales her own mother had spun about long-ago Bourbon kings who built their auxiliary palace there and whiled away their time hunting in La Ficuzza's tangled woods and entertaining in the lush gardens surrounding their palace.

"There are more animals in La Ficuzza than you could ever count," Domenico told his children, "enough to feed Corleone and all the towns in between. In a single day, King Ferdinando could kill as many as a hundred of them. Long before he came here, the *christiani*, their parents, their grandparents, their great-grandparents before them—*everyone* in this area fed their families with game they bagged in those woods. But Ferdinando heard of the riches of this forest and claimed La Ficuzza for himself.

"God protect you if your family's hunger forced you to sneak inside that forest and Ferdinando's guards caught you stealing his game." Domenico slashed the side of his hand hard against his thigh. "Off they'd chop both your hands, then leave you with the blood spurting out of you until you died. Now, say you were hungry enough—or stupid enough—to cut the meat from the flanks of his live cows, thinking you could just sew those dumb animals back up to grow yourself some more meat, then what do you think would happen to you? Well, the king's soldiers would take his branding iron, put it in the fire, and then sear Ferdinando's crest right into your *culo* [behind] so you'd never forget whose meat you had stolen."

Stories of these punishments didn't frighten the children half as much as their father's imitation of La Ficuzza's most ferocious residents, the wild boars. "Eyes alert now," he cautioned, punctuating his words with feral snorts. "If those hungry beasts can't find enough to eat in the forest, they aren't afraid to come looking for a tasty meal."

Tense and wide-eyed silence hung over the back of the cart. Expecting the long-snouted, pointy-tusked monsters to come charging shoulder to shoulder from the distant forest to eat them alive, Rocco, Pasquale, Angelo, and even little Giuseppina concentrated on the distance, staring low.

But try as they might, the children could discern nothing except the massive rock outcroppings that jutted across the valleys undulating in their path. Those mammoth formations punched through the farmland and up toward the sky as if to puncture the rain clouds that hung low with promise across the horizon. Each fall, farm owners and *contadini* alike prayed for rain to sluice away the scorch of summer and succor the thirsty earth. The heavy rains that had started in mid-October had already sparked rejuvenation. Newly coaxed from the summer-parched soil, a carpet of short green grasses glowed in the valleys.

Despite Concetta's fears, the constant rain hadn't washed away the roads. It had made them soggy and much more rutted, and the weary donkeys panted and snorted and strained going uphill. Several times the families had to dismount in the muck while the Costa brothers, sunk to their ankles, heaved their combined brawn against the rear of a cart until they could dislodge its mired wheels and resume the journey. Whenever a sudden cloudburst supplanted the sun, however, Concetta simply threw an extra shawl over her squealing children's heads and directed them to ask God to also soak November.

Without this rain, she admonished, where would they get any wild vegetables to sustain them through the winter and on into spring? Where could she forage any fennel or greens to sauté for an entire meal or to chop fine to give some substance to their thin *minestra*? If it did not keep raining, they would have no wild mushrooms, either, she warned. They could just forget about filling their little mouths with those tasty delicacies.

"A belly growling all winter long is going to feel much worse than an hour sitting with a wet head," she told them. "Trust me, I know."

Shivering, herself, against the chilling drops, she drew baby Francesca closer to her bosom. "Don't complain about getting wet. You just pray to *Dio* to keep sending down this rain, and thank Him that we'll have something to eat in the coming months."

Tired and muddy, at last they arrived in Partinico to a raucous welcome by elderly relatives and cousins, by the relatives of those relatives, and by old friends. Talking all at the same time, the Costas exchanged news and family gossip while those who'd remained in Partinico clucked over the new baby and marveled at how Domenico's and Mario's children had grown. All together, the families went to the church on November 1, the Feast of All Saints, Tutti Santi. The next day, the town awoke to the shrieks of children who ran from their beds to discover that their dead ancestors had not forgotten to bring treats and candies after all. The mothers set the houses in order, brushed their children's hair, gathered up the picnic baskets, and off everyone trooped to the cemetery for the annual *festa*. The men set to uncorking the *vino*, pouring their first drink to clinks of "*Salut*" and "*Cin cin.*" Their children darted around the graves, laughing, chasing, gleeful for the chance to run off the energy bottled up in their short legs during the journey.

The women set to work. With a snap of their wrists they floated brightly hued blankets down in the shadow of the tombstones and began emptying their baskets. With deference, they served the dead first, laying portions of food near their headstones before they set out the special treats reserved for the enjoyment of the dead alone. Children still too little to understand salivated over the delicacies they rarely saw on their own tables, and squawked for a bite of the untouched goodies.

"Didn't you find the special candies that your dear *nonno* brought you while you slept last night?" a mother might ask. "Well, now, in return, we have to give *caro nonno* something wonderful and delicious that is just for him."

"When he was alive," a father might add, "this was his very favorite thing to eat, and it was something he, also, couldn't usually afford to have."

Often the mothers would gently chastise the hungry children, telling them how extra hard their papa had to work to pay for such a small scrap of meat for their deserving *nonno* or *nonna*. Still the children pouted.

"But why can't I have some?" they whined. "Nonno isn't even eating any." Truly, he was, the mothers assured their dubious offspring.

"See, there, that little corner? You can see that part of it is already missing."

The Costas departed from Partinico after the festivities convinced that their decision to relocate had been the right one. If possible, their former town had grown more grungy and their relatives and friends more strapped in the short time since they'd left. Each revolution of their carts' wooden wheels along the rutted roads back to Corleone rolled them that much closer to opportunity, even if the possibility of that new opportunity existed only in the minds of Domenico and Mario and their wives.

Most likely this trip was the last one that my great-grandfather made with Great-Uncle Mario back to Partinico for the Festa dei Morti. The following year, grizzled with grief over the recent deaths of twin sons—one stillborn, his baby brother dead just six months later—Domenico no doubt remained in Corleone to observe the *festa*. With my great-grandmother, he brought the picnic basket and their children to set out candies at the tiny graves of their infant brothers.

That year, my mother told me, Great-Grandma Costa dropped tears on the tombstones, wishing it were her ugly sister Rosalia in the newest grave instead of her sweet Nunzio. It was that beast of a sister who had killed that tiny boy, sure as if she had choked him with her own hands. How dare that witch have shown up at her house as if she were invited, putting Concetta in such a state. Poor little Nunzio never had a chance. Six months old, he died from suckling breast milk that spoiled inside her when she threw the soup pot at her rotten whore of a sister, screaming at Rosalia to leave her house.

Chapter Nine ❧

Detroit, Summer 1916

It was a beautiful dress. A wedding dress fit for any princess who'd graced Ferdinando and Isabella's court at Palermo. The lace on the bodice and sleeves shimmered like flower petals, embellished with countless tiny stitches. The skirt fell in a series of layers, the topmost of which was sheer and edged with horizontal rows of tucking. Sewing late into the night to keep the worry at bay, Concetta crafted Josie's wedding gown from lace and ribbon and yards and yards of fine filmy gauze, all of it purchased with her apron-making earnings.

Though she had begun dreaming of this gown from the moment her eldest daughter first suckled at her breast, Concetta set to drafting the pattern in earnest the morning after Domenic gave Nino permission to seek Josie's hand. Sometimes Josie would keep her company, her crochet hook twirling past bedtime as she crocheted fine multicolored lace around the nightgowns and bed jackets of her *corredo*.

Lips pressed in a grim line above her own needlework, Concetta diverted her thoughts from her husband. As usual, he would return tonight in a haze of grappa and cologne, just as sure as she would shove his discarded shirt into a pillowcase come morning and smuggle it into the basement to scrub out the smears of some other woman's face powder so that her daughters wouldn't have to see it. Domenic was as randy as he'd been in Sicily, still chasing after everything in skirts. Concetta fumed internally as the women in their neighborhood—decent Sicilian *cummari*s, friends who should have sympathized with her—rebuked her. "Can't you take care of that damn husband of yours to keep him at home and away from us?"

Mimicking her older sister, Francesca announced that she wanted to be called Frances. (That didn't sound like much of a change to Agata, who opted to Americanize her name to Aggie. After all, even little Maria's Sicilian school friends only called her Mary now.) Frances sounded older and more sophisticated than Francesca, and twelve-year-old Frances was desperate to be "older." She watched Josie's engagement with fascination and anxiety, finding herself somewhat the odd girl out. She was less than three years away from something so wondrous for herself. With one foot she trailed her adored confidante, who was about to step into a home of her own; with the other, she skipped beside Aggie, who still ran off to play dolls with eight-year-old Mary.

Frances adored Nino and was happy for her sister. Imagine, no matchmaker, just a broom, a porch, and two young people swept off their feet! The two inseparable sisters talked of Josie's luck in adoring a man who had an equal passion for her, when so often they had watched other girls forced by their parents into loveless matches. That practice of arranged marriage was not left behind in Sicily; it was carried across the ocean by the immigrants who settled in Detroit. Josie and Frances knew luckless girls, daughters of *cummari*s who had betrothed them to brutes, sometimes much older brutes, promising the hapless girls that love would come later. Yet even as those parents promised, they knew it wasn't always so. To Josie and Frances, the attentions of a man one was smitten with was the ultimate in romance and *fortuna*.

Yet happy as she was for Josie, Frances couldn't escape feeling somewhat sad for herself. Not only was her dearest friend leaving her in a few months, she had already begun to pull away. With conflicted feelings, Frances savored every minute, every whisper, every evening of embroidery that she shared with her closest sister. For once Josie married Nino, the two sisters would see each other only on Sundays, and their relationship would be radically changed. Sisters or no, Josie would graduate to the congregation of married women and Frances would be left behind on the other side of the room with all the girls.

Josie had outpaced her on the track to womanhood, growing breasts and sprouting pubic hair and having to wear torn strips of old bed sheets between her legs once a month like Mama did. Frances had a hair or two in her armpits, but while the girls dressed in the morning, she could see that the bumps on her chest still looked more like Aggie's than Josie's. At night, when she lay in bed saying her prayers, she fantasized about a wedding of her own, wondering who would come up the front stairs to ask Papa if he could court *her*. Josie lay beside her, clueless about the tingles that tickled low in her belly whenever she thought about her Nino. My grandmother told me just what an innocent she'd been. No one even hinted to her about sex. The only thing Josie knew about married life was that soon they would live together and she would wash his clothes and cook him pasta.

Nino and Josie brushed fingers only once during their year-long courtship, just long enough for him to slide the small diamond engagement ring onto her left hand while her parents and siblings hovered at their elbows to inspect.

The engagement—their *conuscenza*—was formalized with a party at the Costa home to which all their friends, relatives, neighbors, *cummari*s, and *cumpari*s were invited. Concetta served their guests various cakes and glasses of wine, and everyone toasted the newly engaged *fidanzati* and wished them *bona fortuna*. That afternoon the two sat side by side, but still apart, beaming at each other and their well-wishers, but not even allowed to hold each other's hand. With marriage now near, the two would find themselves chaperoned even more closely, lest the anticipation of approaching intimacy send hormones racing uncontrolled.

Although Sicilian adults have always been open and enthusiastic commentators on sexual matters, like most young Sicilian girls, Josie and Frances and their younger sisters were kept in complete ignorance about love and sex. Married women's knowing winks and innuendo-filled repartee about sexual pleasures sailed right over young girls' heads, right down to the jokes about the kneading board. After the wedding night, no young bride ever again pumped her board's attached kneading arm without thinking about the rhythm of intercourse.

Innocent as they were, Josie and Frances found men fascinating, and envied what they believed to be their great adventures out in the world. The sisters thought their older brothers suave, debonair, and mysterious, with their dandy clothes and their worldly friends who drove up to the Costas' home in flashy cars. While neither of the girls could step onto the front porch without the other, and never off that porch without an adult chaperoning them, their brothers were at liberty to come and go at will, often staying away from home for days at a time.

To think that, with such limitations on her activity, Josie's own true love would come walking right down her street! Truly, America was a wondrous place, even for a Sicilian girl.

Back in Mazara del Vallo, Giovannina played a vicarious role in her son's engagement. Having known poverty himself, it pained Nino to learn that, desperate to buy bread for her hungry family, Concetta had once stolen Josie's gold earrings and sold them while she slept. Nino promised himself that he'd always have enough money to buy Josie jewelry. Every month, along with the money he sent to his mother, he enclosed extra so that she could purchase Josie another ring and another, until she had sent Nino twelve different gold rings—each one set with a different month's birthstone. Some were delicate, some were large, each was different and beautiful in its own right.

For Thanksgiving, he gave her a large champagne-colored topaz that popped from a slim band. For Christmas, it was a square turquoise stone offset with two tiny diamonds. In February, her birthday amethyst was small and the setting delicate. The May emerald was centered between two pinpoint pearls in an oval setting of antiqued scrollwork. Josie tucked the ring boxes inside the top drawer of the bedroom dresser, for she could only wear one ring on her left hand at a time. Sometimes during Mass, Concetta would glance over at the gemstones sparkling like stained glass on her eldest daughter's fingers and she'd thank God that Josie wouldn't have to steal *her* daughter's jewelry in the middle of the night to buy her family bread. Yes, she thought, America was a better life for her daughters.

Chapter Ten ❧

Corleone, 1906

Like most Sicilians and Italians from the southern region of the boot, the Costas dispatched their prayers, petitions, and praise to heaven through the saints. Weighed down with thanksgiving offerings of gold and silver jewelry, coins and paper money, these gilded emissaries still stand ensconced in church alcoves, shimmering in the flicker of the votive candles lit at their feet to remind them of their missions.

Outdoors, omnipresent Madonnas and saints peek out everywhere you turn, keeping watch over daily life from little grottoes tucked into walls and stuffed with tokens, candles, and flowers.

Downtrodden and demoralized by centuries of a powerless feudal existence, with no say about which conqueror was governing them that century, Sicilian peasants like the Costas and their ancestors took seriously their only stab at democracy—organizing, campaigning, and voting into "office" the community's patron saint. Enshrined and beloved if all went well, the saint would be insulted and vilified if things did not. If the harvest was short, the donkey went lame, the barn burned down, the milk soured, the saint's statue would be turned to face the wall, moved outside, flung to the ground, spit upon, sworn at, or stomped on in rebuke. If a town's collective prayers went unanswered time after time, the call of wildly ringing church bells would send the aggrieved villagers running to the square to publicly denounce their saint. Exercising the only enfranchisement they possessed, they'd cast their ballots and vote the vilified patron out of office.

Concetta Lupica's devotion was always to the Virgin Mary. Her children later credited her faith in the Holy Mother with saving their father's life and with mystically setting into motion the religious course their youngest brothers' lives would take years later in America.

In 1906 Domenico was a horse salesman, a sales job that, like most of the others he held in Sicily, meant he was often absent from home for several days at time. Since most peasants could barely afford to buy and maintain the donkeys they depended on to help them farm, there was no local business for horse traders. Breeders raised the horses in the country, and salesmen like Domenico helped break them, train them, and take them to prospective buyers in the large cities, like Palermo. They also armed themselves and slept with one eye open to watch for the thieves who could steal three horses and sell them one hundred miles away before an owner knew they were missing.

It was early in December, and Concetta, as usual, was scraping for some dinner to feed their six children. She put two-year-old Agata down to nap and sent the boys off with a sack to forage in the hills nearby for broccoli, cabbage, or whatever vegetables they could find at this time of year. Most of the wild greens would have already been harvested by scavengers who'd set off at four or five in the morning and stuffed their sacks with as much as they could find and carry home. Some they'd eat themselves, most they'd hand to their wives to wash clean so the middlemen would be more likely to pay them a few cents a bunch.

Her belly eight months swollen with an active baby, Concetta had been spending the majority of her days wrapped in her light wool shawl, seated just outside the small stone house. While she visited with the neighbor women and worked on embroidering a tablecloth, she'd begun to teach Giuseppina, almost six years old, how to thread a needle. Needlework like this was usually done in the cooler months, since the intense summers made for sweaty hands on fabric. Giuseppina and Francesca, who was three, huddled at their mother's knees while she sewed. Using their pudgy little elbows to gain purchase on her lap, the two curly-haired sisters hoisted themselves on their toes and leaned in to watch Concetta's needle fly through the white cloth.

The late fall afternoon was warm and clear and the fabric glowed in the sunlight. Crowding against her knees, Concetta's little girls squinted at the tiny white flowers that trailed like magic in the shiny wake of their mother's needle.

Domenico and the other horsemen watched the storm clouds gathering darker and larger to the north of Palermo, nearer the bay. Rain had threatened all morning, but so far—in the southern outskirts of the city where they were working the horses—the weather had held. Now the clouds were growing so rapidly it looked as if they were sucking water from the bay as they scuttled over it on their way inland. The horses had sensed the approaching storm before the men had and had been skittish for nearly an hour, paying less and less heed to their trainers. Domenico had picked up on it first, noticing the way the mare he was working with kept flicking her ears back, afraid.

It became increasingly difficult for the men to keep the horses on task, but a storm still out over the bay was not excuse enough to bring them in to shelter. Their boss expected these animals to be ready for market. One stomping a hoof, another one nickering, the horses began to circle closer together. One by one, they turned their rumps to the north as the wind picked up. The trainers pulled them apart.

Domenico eyed the nasty clouds. It wouldn't be the first time they'd have to keep working in a driving rain.

Soon it became so dark out to the north, the men could not discern where the low clouds ended and the slashing rain began. The horses began to run in a lopsided circle as the first rumbles of thunder rolled in from the bay. They reared and whinnied, wild-eyed, when the first sharp snap of lightning cut across the sky. Together, they began to run.

Lightning unzipped the sky and thunder roared its approval. Rain, cold and spitting, stung the men's faces and hands. A number of horses tore for shelter, following the mare's lead. Domenico hung hard to the reins of his powerful animal, straining to keep it from bolting. Others shouted after the horses as they took off in fast pursuit. Once they could recapture them, they still had a hard five-minute ride back to the stables.

Domenico was within shouting distance of the rickety stables when a sword of light ripped out of heaven, seized him by the shoulder, and threw him from his horse. His terror-stricken animal charged toward the stable, fleeing the rider crumpled facedown in the muck.

Fearing the worst, Mario dashed to his brother. Another horseman was at his heels. The two men rolled Domenico over and saw that he was not breathing. His woolen shirt was charred and smoking, its fibers fused to the blisters raised red and weeping where the lightning had sizzled into Domenico's shoulder and then down his chest. His left hand was swollen red and black, as if he'd held it too long over a blazing fire. Together, the men dragged him into the stables, lay him on the straw, and began removing his shirt. They ripped open his long sleeves and cringed at what they found. The fabric had concealed Domenico's additional injuries. His left arm was a raw and oozing mess, seared from the shoulder to the fingertips.

Mario yelled his brother's name, slapping him repeatedly on the face. Nothing. He scooped a tin cup into the horses' water trough and dribbled some into his brother's mouth. Another of the horsemen ran to bring a bottle of grappa, but that, too, only filled Domenico's mouth and then puddled onto his chest.

Finally, one of the men gripped Mario by the shoulder. "There is nothing more we can do for him in this world but send someone to bring him his wife."

The old men who passed their days playing endless games of *scopa* in the town square saw the lone rider first. He rode hard up the rocky terrain, and stopped his panting horse and their card game only long enough to inquire as to the direction of Domenico Costa's house.

The children on his route ran from their mothers' skirts to watch the gleaming dark beast chasing down their narrow cobbled streets. Most of them had watched the horse races from behind the barricades during the annual *festa* of San Leoluca, Corleone's patron saint, but had never been this close to a horse before. Many were from families too poor to own a mule, let alone a horse. Concetta's children ventured into the street to witness the excitement. They were both startled and filled with awe when the mysterious rider stopped short just outside their little home.

He removed his brimmed felt hat, revealing a sun-leathered face.

"*Mi dispiace, signora.* Your husband is dead. Bring his burial clothes and I will take you to Palermo."

For a moment, the blood drained from Concetta's face. It pooled in her vocal cords and then throbbed out a piercing wail. Her children burst into tears, but Concetta was oblivious to their fright. She dropped her needlework and bolted. Her children scurried after her like a trail of terrified ducklings as she ran for the nearest church, screeching to the Virgin Mary all the way there.

Concetta barged through the heavy wooden doors and lumbered toward the Virgin's alcove. Pressing her giant belly into the altar in front of the Madonna's statue, she flung her arms across the crocheted altar cloth and soaked it with her tears.

"Oh, Madonna, bring my husband back to life and I promise to dedicate to your Son any more babies that Domenico gives me. Holy Virgin, help me. What can I do with seven children? Bring my husband back to life and I will give my earrings to the church."

"Mama! Papa!" Red-faced with tears, the Costa children clamored for comfort, pulling at her skirt. By then, the neighborhood women had flocked to the church to help Concetta wail and pray. So intent were these women on their supplications that not one of them stooped to soothe the little ones jumping around their mother.

Finally, Concetta's sister-in-law, Wanda, coaxed her up from the altar and led her home to the waiting messenger. Wanda pulled from the wooden *cassete* Concetta's one good dress, basic, black, and reserved for bereavement. They could not begin to tug it over her swollen breasts and belly. Concetta wrapped herself instead in a black shawl and handed her children off to Wanda.

Concetta's journey to Palermo was an arduous one—she had to follow her mounted escort on foot. Peasant women were accustomed to walking behind the donkeys their husbands rode, and often did so while carrying heavy loads on their heads. Besides, decorum wouldn't permit her to ride beside the escort on his horse, even if she hadn't been too far along in her pregnancy to mount it. By the time she rounded the hallway to the hospital morgue the following day, her feet were swollen and blistered and she was beyond exhaustion.

Concetta staggered into the room where Mario stood watch over his brother's body. She saw Mario in his mourning cloak, and then Domenico arrayed in death—his feet pointed toward the door, his mouth tied closed with black ribbon looped under his chin and knotted at the top of his head, his cot strewn with oleander leaves—and she burst into hysteria. Mario took up the mourning chant as Concetta flew across the room. She flung herself across her husband's body and began to scream all the louder. In that same instant, crazed with hideous pain, her dead Domenico bellowed himself back to life.

"Amazing!" the doctors marveled, as Mario shrugged off his mourning cloak. "An extreme case of shock."

But Concetta knew otherwise. The Madonna had delivered Domenico from the dead and she owed the Virgin her gold earrings—and Jesus any children she delivered after this one.

For twenty-four days and nights, she never left Domenico's side. She fed him, she bathed him, she demanded that he get well. His contracted right forearm bent at the elbow like a chicken's wing, pulling his clenched fist to within an inch of his shoulder. His forearm muscles and biceps were raw and oozing. When the lymph crystalized to a honeylike substance and fused the two limbs together, Concetta plied them apart while Domenico screamed. His burns became infected and the pain more excruciating. He mumbled from delirium and sweated profusely from fever, my grandmother told me. Despite her cumbersome belly, Concetta hoisted her husband off his mattress and shuttled him single-handedly from one bed to another, moving him from the sweat-soaked linens to try to cool him down.

Christmas brought no celebration, and by the end of those first twenty-four days, the doctors came to Concetta and told her they must amputate Domenico's shriveled and infected arm. She was having none of it, though her brother-in-law, Mario, tried to persuade her to defer to the doctors.

"Everyone covers up the doctor's mistakes," she told him. *"Lu medicu e' coma la boja: si paga pr'ammazzari!"* The doctor is like the butcher: you pay him to kill!

She wasn't going to let any doctor kill her husband, now that he was back from the dead. Again, she turned to the Virgin Mary and bargained.

"Oh, Madonna *mia,* I beg you, spare my Domenico his arm and if this baby is a girl I will name her Maria after you, or name him Giuseppe, after your husband, if he's a boy."

A few days later, on the second of January 1907, Concetta went into labor. She produced another daughter, a dark-haired infant born with one arm shorter than the other and with a lazy eye. Within a minute of the delivery, she named the baby Maria.

Concetta's bargain with the Holy Mother proved a worthy one. Although it took three operations and an entire year, the doctors in Palermo did manage to save Domenico's gnarled right arm. For that entire year, Concetta worked on her husband's arm, too. Bound and determined that he would use the contracted limb again, she concocted a regimen far ahead of its time. Using straps and rope and anything of heft she could find—a book, a hammer, a jug—she tied the weight to Domenico's wrist or to his arm and then she attacked that limb like a twenty-first-century physical therapist. Up and down, side to side, she stretched and pulled and chided him through the pain. With each measure of progress, Concetta increased the weight. Relentlessly, without mercy, she forced the scarred and fused tissues to stretch.

It was one of the worst years of Concetta's life. She was chained to a new baby and a seriously injured husband, both of them totally dependent upon her. She barely had the wherewithal to think about her other six children, left to the generosity of Domenico's family in Corleone, and no energy with which to miss them. She existed in a constant state of anxiety and fear. Her family was destitute, and what little food they did eat meant that much less for the family members sustaining them. Most days, no matter how strenuously she worked her husband's arm, the doctors warned her that Domenico might never be able to support his family again.

But with seven children to raise, Concetta refused to concede defeat. She had tenacity and she had her Madonna, and she called upon both.

By the following November, the Costa family had finally settled back into their own small home in Corleone. They were penniless, Concetta was once again pregnant, but she'd managed to coax Domenico's arm back to within four inches of its former length.

Chapter Eleven ❧

My great-grandfather Domenico Costa.

Domenico didn't return to working the horses, but he couldn't go back to the wheat fields, either. After tasting the travel, the banter, and the facade of freedom that came with a job in sales, Domenico decided to try his hand at selling flour. He became a middleman between the land baron and the housewives, traveling the countryside peddling the fine durum farina ground out in the landowner's mill.

Each Monday, the older boys, Rocco, Pasquale, and Angelo,

walked off with a chunk of bread and grim faces to begin another week in the wheat fields. Each Monday, their father left Corleone with a happy whistle to cart flour. Since the mill owners would only sell to salesmen who belonged to the carters' association, Domenico had joined. Contrary to Italy's commercial laws against price-fixing, first the mill owners and then later the carters had organized to prevent price wars and competitive undercutting. For this "protection," Domenico had to pay the association a *posa*, or tax, on every cart of flour he carried away from the mill. At the start of each week, he would drive his donkey cart to the mill, load it high with the small sacks of flour, then set off down the hill with his dancing pallet wedged in behind him. For the better part of the week, Domenico would travel the surrounding towns and villages, selling his flour by the kilo or by the cup, according to what each housewife could afford. My grandmother told us that, on occasion, her father was only too glad to work out other arrangements with a willing housewife, if time and circumstance permitted.

He knew too well his sons' work in the fields and was glad to be at the other end of the production chain. He still had to pay the landholder (through his *gabellotto*, the middleman who managed the farm) for the grain the boys sowed, still had to keep their tools sharpened and in good order, but he no longer had to sweat with them under the hot sun from predawn to dusk.

Each morning, knapsack in one hand, hoe in the other, Rocco, Pasquale, and Angelo knocked on the door of the *gabellotto*, or of his field guards, the *campieri*, to buy the day's seed. Seed was always purchased while the guardian star of dawn, Lucifer, still twinkled in the inky heavens. By its light they scrutinized the transaction with a measure of anxiety, for they had no recourse if they were cheated, or "taken for *fesso*." The wealthy landlords lived in distant cities. They divided their land into parcels and left the day-to-day operations to the *gabellotti* and *campieri*. For the pleasure of eking out an existence with such grueling labor, the *contadini* had to pay the *gabellotti* with the best of the harvest, anywhere from two to four and a half bushels of wheat per acre, which often amounted to half the acre's production. Since the *contadini* had to borrow from the same *gabellotti* in order to purchase the seeds—usually at an interest rate of 50 percent—most of them could never get ahead. They subsisted in a feudal system that solely benefited the landlord and his hirelings. Almost without exception, the *gabellotti* employed a different weighing standard for the seed they sold the *contadino* and the harvested wheat they credited to him, measuring heavy when selling the seed and light at harvest time.

No, Domenico had had enough of the fields, the backbreaking labor, the blistered calluses, the constant salt of sweat in his eyes. The itinerant life was more to his liking. Wanderlust—or perhaps lust all by itself—pulsed through his veins. Besides, Domenico possessed *furberia*—shrewdness or cleverness. As he made his rounds with his sacks of farina, it would not be Domenico who'd be taken for *fesso*.

The larger cities had outdoor markets where the vendors hawked their wares from stalls. The small villages had the itinerant vendors, who brought goods along with gossip from the villages along their route. There was camaraderie among the merchants who traveled the countryside, plying their wares from town to town. Their voices preceded them into a town and they could trill out the praises of their merchandise just as entertainingly as the city vendors who outshouted each other in the marketplace, persuading customers away from a competitor with a clever spiel.

There was the water seller, *lu paracquaru,* with his clay jugs suspended from the pole he balanced across his shoulders as he called out, "The water has arrived! Such beautiful, fresh water!" *L'uvara,* the egg lady, would visit three times a week, with her wicker baskets balanced alternately on hip or head and filled with the eggs she had collected from the house chickens of her *cummaris.* There were vendors of clothing, shoes, green beans, vegetables, and fruit in their season, of fish and kitchen utensils and pots. In larger cities there were even *lu cafiterri,* who paraded down the streets early in the morning and again at night, selling little cups of sweetened strong coffee.

Giuseppina's household chores, and then Francesca's, increased as they began to learn women's skills. Each week, after Concetta folded the bed linens and towels she hung outside to air-dry, she handed over the pile to Giuseppina to put away in the long chest of drawers kept in the parents' bedroom.

Giuseppina discovered several small fragrant apples tucked inside the linen drawer, but her mother refused to let her eat any of them. "No apples," Concetta told her. "I don't have enough for everyone, and the reason I put them there is to make our linens smell good. Back to your needlework now."

But Giuseppina's mouth watered every week when she opened the wooden dresser redolent with apples. Finally she could stand it no longer. Glancing around to make certain that no one could see her, Giuseppina snatched one from beneath the linens and chomped off a little bite. Her heart pounding, she slid the apple back under the sheets, bitten side down.

For the next several weeks, Giuseppina rushed to help her mother with the linens, anxious for the chance to sneak herself a little treat. One afternoon when a blanket had taken longer than usual to dry, Concetta waited to fold it and then decided to put it away herself. Giuseppina was playing with Francesca when their mother screamed for her to come immediately to the bedroom. The seven-year-old knew that Mama had found the browned, bitten apples.

Lips compressed in a scowl, Concetta yanked her eldest daughter toward her and waved a shriveled, tooth-marked piece of fruit in her face.

"My apples," she screamed, bashing the fruit against Giuseppina's mouth. "You want to eat my apples? Good." Again and again, she slammed the bloody apple into her daughter's teeth as Giuseppina struggled to wrest herself free of her mother's grip.

"*Perduno,* Mama, *perduno,*" she sobbed. "Pardon." But forgiveness was not on Concetta's mind. She could be as brutal as her husband.

"Here," Concetta screamed, bashing at her little girl's face while Francesca cowered outside the doorway in tears. "Go ahead. Eat my apples." She threw the blood-soaked apple to the floor only after she had knocked out both of Giuseppina's top teeth.

Although Concetta couldn't afford to serve her children apples, Domenico's family was still well fed in the years he peddled farina. Not because he was industrious. Not because he made a lot of money selling flour. Bread was plentiful on the Costa table because Domenico had big hands. When he emptied the contents of his flour sacks into the housewives' larders, he would grab up the sack by its two bottom corners, trapping handfuls of flour inside. He'd shake out the bag until it was "empty," and the housewife would believe she got full measure. When she counted out the coins she'd scraped together to keep her family nourished, she never suspected she was paying Domenico for the two cups of flour he was taking home to his wife. There wasn't a *contadina* in all of Sicily who would have believed that another peasant would stoop so low as to make *fesso* of one of his own.

Domenico had no qualms about shortchanging his customers, however, for Sicilians believed that stealing something for need was not stealing unless what you took exceeded your need. His family needed bread, didn't it? And wasn't it the Lord Himself who said, "Help yourselves as I help you?"

"*Cu' arrobba pri mangiari, nun fa piccatu.*" Concetta would mutter the Sicilian proverb when he handed her the flour. "Who steals to eat isn't a sinner."

Chapter Twelve ❧

Corleone, 1910

Francesca, like all her Italian-born siblings, attended school for only a single year—just long enough to learn the alphabet and the rudiments of writing and reading. Compulsory education for children between the ages of six and nine had become the law throughout Italy in 1877, but few peasant children, especially Sicilian peasant children, ever attended school for three years. Communities in southern Italy and Sicily often appropriated for other purposes any monies earmarked for building schools. Teachers were appointed, supplies were limited, and peasants weren't all that interested in having their children learn to read and write. Their sons could not be spared from the fieldwork and their daughters were destined to become homebound housewives. The girls needed to sit with their mothers, aunts, and older sisters and learn to sew, embroider, weave, cook, and tend the house.

By the age of seven, childhood was over for Francesca and her sisters. Like all Southern Italian girls, they had to set to work learning to become women, and the first thing they learned was how to embroider simple stitches and to weave. Entire days were spent at the little looms, and then at bigger ones, for a girl usually had less than ten years to weave and embroider and sew her *corredo* and wedding trousseau. Once engaged, a young *fidanzata* had to make herself a shawl, several good dresses, several everyday dresses and aprons, the table and bed linens for her new home, and the simple shirt and trousers she must sew for her future husband and present to him just before the wedding.

Since skill at their weaving and sewing would net them a better marriage, the Costa girls had to learn to make many kinds of fabrics. *Rigatino,* a striped cloth from which girls sewed their own clothing, was the first they tackled. For men's wear they learned to weave fustian and *tela,* a homespun linen also used to make everyday underwear, shirts, and sheets. Finally, they acquired the skill to create the finest fabric of all, an exquisite linen called *alessandrina.* They learned to sew and to cook and how to knead the bread dough by pressing down on it with the thick wooden handle that was attached to the special kneading board. Sometimes, when the only flour they could afford to buy for making bread was corn flour or one extracted from ground beans, they had to press on that dough extra hard. They memorized the recipes for holiday cookies, and even learned how to take an extra bit of flour and an extra egg from the larder and turn them into hand-cut pasta. Hardest of all their culinary tasks, however, was the annual preparation of *'u 'strattu,* the dense tomato extract that Sicilian women rendered from the tomato harvest.

At the height of each summer, Giuseppina and Francesca and their sisters would help the older women make this concentrated tomato paste. First they had to wash, slice, and peel the ripe tomatoes, then lay them outside to dry by scattering the fruit across large wooden boards supported by sawhorses. These makeshift tables were slanted, one end set lower than the other so that the juices and tomato seeds could easily drain off. Each day the women stood under the relentless sun and stirred the drying pulp with large wooden paddles, shooing away the flies with one hand while using the other to constantly turn the tomatoes so that every surface was equally exposed to the sun and hot summer air. Each night the women and the tomatoes rested.

As the tomatoes dried, their volume condensed, their color deepened, and their flavor intensified. If the Costas could afford salt, they would sprinkle some across the *'strattu.* After several days of constant stirring, spreading, stirring, the women's three tables of tomatoes would have shrunk in volume to fill just one. Then the most grueling part of making the *'strattu* began. By this stage, the paste was thicker, denser, redder, and harder to push and pull, spread and stir. When the *'strattu* was finally thick enough to mold like dough, it was finished. Then the women oiled their hands and packed the brick-red paste tightly into earthen jars, "sealing" the *'strattu* by drizzling first a thin layer of oil across the top, then a layer of salt, before finally covering the jar with cloth.

It was exhausting, but the women knew their work was worth it. Even a tiny teaspoon of the precious paste enriched the flavor of anything they cooked.

The year before Francesca started school, the streak of girls born into Domenico Costa's family ended. After four consecutive daughters, Concetta gave birth to Luigi. As an old man in America, he would tell his great-nieces that his godfather had been the mayor of Corleone and the head of the local Mafia.

Soon his big sisters had still another baby brother to dote on. The year after Francesca ended her brief formal education, Salvatore arrived to bump Luigi out of their parents' bedroom and up into the loft with the seven other siblings.

If the arrival of the boy babies was a source of entertainment or joy for the Costa daughters, being sandwiched between them and the older three brothers was not. Domenico was now working as a wine taster and away from the house for longer periods than when he had worked the fields or broken and sold horses or simply gone off with his dance pallet to carouse. Rocco took upon himself the role of surrogate father. Pasquale and Angelo, too, made demands on their sisters for food and clean clothes, but Rocco took special pleasure in assuming the position of undisputed authority. He was fifteen, swimming in testosterone, and full of himself. He'd grown up watching his father occasionally belt his mother, or his uncle belt his aunt, and the neighbors belt their wives. Swaggering about the house in his father's absence, Rocco took delight in dishing out orders, deferring authority only to his Zio Mario.

While Rocco stopped short of ever laying a hand on his mother, he considered the donkey, the dog, and his sisters fair game. A pinch here, a slap or kick there, and Giuseppina, Francesca, Agata, and Maria served well as target practice for Rocco's future skills as a husband. The dog could always dart under the table or scoot out the door. His sisters weren't always that lucky.

Having watched their mother's belly swell with Luigi and Salvatore, Francesca and her sisters soon became fixated on their dog, Bruna, when her bloating belly and swollen teats broadcast that puppies were on the way.

Bruna grew wider, her teats hung lower, and the mama dog steered clear of Rocco and his swift feet. One morning, long after the boys had left for work, she waddled out the door and disappeared for such a long time that the girls began to call after her. Concetta directed them back to their sewing, telling them that Bruna had most likely wandered off to find herself a quiet spot to birth her puppies.

That was it. None of the girls could keep their attention on their stitches. All they could think about was finding Bruna's hiding place and those newborn puppies.

Finally Concetta let them go and the four sisters went squealing off down the street with several of the neighbor children. A commotion of little voices went up when they discovered Bruna nuzzling and licking six sleepy puppies that more resembled little mice without tails. They were snug against the back of a neighbor's stone house, where Bruna had given birth on a patch of dirt strewn with straw and shaded by a canopy of grapevines.

"Leave them be," the old man who lived in the house called out to the children crowding around Bruna and her puppies for a better look. "Leave her babies alone or she's gonna take a bite out of you." The children ran home to report the news, and the four Costa girls could barely contain themselves until their brothers got home from the fields and they could tell them all about Bruna's funny little puppies.

"Pasquale, Angelo, *veni ca,* come quickly!" Francesca jumped up and called to her brothers the minute she spotted them heading up the street. "The puppies. They're behind Signore Cimino's. Come see Bruna's puppies before supper. They are so cute, like little drunk mice without any hair."

"Puppies, you say?" Angelo greeted her with a tug on her long chestnut braid as she caught up to them. "All this excitement over a few new puppies?"

"We'll show them to you, Rocco," she called. Wordlessly, her eldest brother trudged past his little sisters, heading straight for the small stone house. Only as he reached their doorway did he turn toward Francesca.

"Get in and help Mama and Giuseppina serve the meal. Or did you forget we've been in the fields breaking our backs all day on just bread and onions? There are already plenty of mouths to feed around here without having to go look at any more."

Francesca lowered her eyes and quickly scurried inside after him. Concetta was setting the bowls of *minestra* on the wooden table while baby Salvatore hung on her leg, howling like an injured animal.

"Go, Francesca," her mother said. "Help Giuseppina pour your brothers some water while I get him quiet. Rocco won't be happy with a screaming baby at the table."

Angelo grabbed her elbow as she set a cup of water next to his bowl. "After we eat, I'll go see the puppies with you," he whispered. "I promise."

"Truly?" Francesca smiled shyly, still self-conscious about her two missing baby teeth.

"Truly."

"Keep moving, Francesca," Pasquale ordered. "Angelo's not the only one who's thirsty."

While their mother sat in the corner to nurse little Salvatore, the sisters, eleven and eight, fed their brothers and sisters, jumping up from their own suppers to refill bowls and cups until finally the last brother pushed himself back from the table with a satisfied belch, leaving the girls to clean up.

"Now, does anyone here know something about little bald mice running around drunk behind Signore Cimino's?" Angelo asked. Before Francesca had a chance to turn from the stack of bowls and spoons to answer him, Angelo swooped her up. She shrieked with delight as he hoisted her up onto his back and spun her around the table. At thirteen, Angelo swaggered more and mimicked his older brothers when he was around them, but Francesca still saw flashes of childhood in her third brother. Laughing, she hung on to his head as best she could and yelled out for him to duck so she wouldn't smack her head on the door frame as he ran with her out of the house.

The two of them were breathless from laughter by the time they ran up the nearby narrow street where Signore Cimino lived. They could hear Bruna's high-pitched barking echoing from the rear of the small house as they rounded it, and from her shoulder-high perch Francesca could see that someone else had come to visit the puppies, too.

"Rocco! Oh, you did come to see the puppies," she cried, as Angelo came up behind their eldest brother. Rocco turned to regard them, one tiny puppy clenched head down in his beefy fist. In the same instant, Francesca spotted the others. They were littered at his feet, while their mother ran back and forth, barking and yapping and nudging at their broken bodies with her nose.

"No!" Francesca screamed, struggling to climb down from Angelo's shoulders. "Rocco, no!"

But it was too late. Easy as cracking open a chestnut, her brother smashed the last puppy's head against Signore Cimino's house with a single slam and then he tossed it, lifeless, to the ground.

"Angelo!" He barked his younger brother's name like an order. "Why isn't she home doing the supper dishes? It's time all the females were inside the house."

Francesca wanted desperately to jump down from Angelo's back and pummel Rocco with her fists, but she couldn't even summon the strength to glance in his direction. She buried her face in Angelo's hair instead, soaking it with tears.

Chapter Thirteen ❧

The photo my mother told me was my grandparents' wedding photo.

Detroit, 1916

Although at home Domenic's children spoke Sicilian almost
exclusively, the younger ones came home from school with
ink-stained fingers and tried to teach him and Concetta some English words, mostly in hopes that their parents would no longer
embarrass them when they shopped in non-Italian stores. Stores

were still a novelty to Concetta and her daughters. Imagine! Going to the merchant yourself, rather than waiting until an itinerant merchant came to you.

Sure, some things were still sold door-to-door, same as in Sicily. Milk, for example, or ice, which the iceman brought several times a week. Concetta had to remember to have her children write either a "5" or a "10" on a piece of cardboard to prop in the window so he'd know how many pounds of it she wanted hauled into her kitchen and placed under the lid of the metal-lined wooden icebox that kept their food chilled. But butcher markets and greengrocers sat in the middle of neighborhoods, nestled on the side streets right between houses. If Concetta ran out of sugar, she'd just send Josie and Frances six houses down the block to buy it while she watched from the front porch. Eastern Market was close enough that Domenic or one of her sons or Nino could carry in fresh produce. And when she wanted to cook a chicken for dinner, Concetta just had to walk down the back stairs into her yard and wring its neck herself.

As the months went by, Frances watched the linens and garments for Josie's trousseau pile up in her sister's *cassete*. The wedding dress was finished. It waited at the back of the closet while Concetta sewed silk lilies of the valley to the headpiece of Josie's matching multilayered veil. Next she would start on the party dresses for her other daughters, with dropped waists and half-sleeves, while she thought about one for herself. In just a few months, everyone they knew would fill Holy Family Church for the wedding and then spend several days celebrating in the Costas' backyard.

In some ways, Frances relished the fact that soon she would be the eldest girl at home, more closely shadowing her mother in preparation for her own marriage someday. But she dreaded the increased responsibility for her older brothers' laundry. Rocco, especially, wasn't above a push or a slap to punctuate his disapproval. She envied her younger sisters the time they spent away from the house in school.

May and June and July brought Josie three more engagement rings and more frequent visits from her fiancé. Now, in addition to Sunday dinner, Nino sat at his future in-laws' table at least one weeknight. Josie was helping him compose his letters to Giovannina in Sicily now, writing in her curved European script. As they sat across the table from each other, the young couple's talk was turning more toward their future as the wedding date neared.

Nino was looking for a flat to rent and putting aside as much as he could spare to save for a house, and Josie was completing her trousseau. By mid-August she had nearly finished sewing her nightclothes and was anxious for Nino to try on the pants she was expected to sew for him so that she could hem them properly.

One Sunday, as they dipped biscotti into small glasses of wine and cracked walnuts, almonds, and filberts for dessert, Domenic and Nino began preliminary discussions about the wedding feast, with Concetta and Josie chiming in. It was excited, happy conversation, only slightly diminished by Nino's regret that his mother and sister could not be with them on their wedding day. Perhaps, when he could afford the trip, he said, he would take Josie to Mazara to meet his family.

As the afternoon waned, Nino bid the Costas good-bye and rose from the table to head for home, with Josie a few steps behind him. He was halfway down the front steps when the sun beating down on him reminded Nino that he'd left his straw hat inside. He hadn't taken one step back when Josie spied it still perched on the wooden coatrack in the front hallway. Without thinking, she whipped the hat off the rack, and as Nino opened the front door, she stretched her arm through the opening and handed his hat to him, just as her father stepped into the hallway behind her.

"*Puttana!*" he screamed ("Whore!"), and in an instant he was on her, his hand gripped like a vise around her wrist. He yanked Josie from the door, which slammed shut behind her, separating the couple. The force of his pull sent her crashing into the staircase, even as her father barged through the front door to face down Nino on the front porch.

"This engagement is canceled!" he bellowed, spittle flying from the corners of his moustache. "Don't you ever show your face in this house again."

"No!" Sobbing, Josie twisted toward the door, catching one last glimpse of Nino. His eyes narrowed and his jaw clenched, and then he whirled around and hurried down the stairs.

"Finished!" Domenic bellowed at Nino's back.

The pain in Josie's heart screamed more than in her ribcage. Domenic slammed the front door and grabbed Josie by the arm, dragging her, wild-eyed and sobbing, down the hallway to the back door where he kept the dog's chain. He tore the metal leash from the hook and began flailing on Josie, beating her on her arms, her back, her head, her buttocks, her legs, as he dragged her down the hallway and up the stairs while his wife and younger children cowered.

"You blacken the face of this family?"

"No, Papa, no. Please——"

The welts were already an angry purple when he threw her onto her bed and began tying her to it with the dog chain.

"You filthy whore! Is this what you learn in America? I'll teach you how a good girl behaves. Finished! You hear me?"

He slammed the bedroom door so hard her ears hurt.

"This engagement is *finished.*"

Huddled over the kitchen sink, Concetta and Frances listened to Josie's wracking sobs and their own tears helped rinse the dishes they washed. Frances hung her head, terrified to meet her father's eyes when he stormed into the kitchen, thundering at Concetta that Josie was no longer engaged. She tried not to tremble, but her stomach was still knotted from the metallic slaps of the dog chain and her sister's cries. She'd seen her father beat her mother, and had herself suffered blows from Rocco, but she had never—ever—seen her father lay a hand on any of his four daughters until today. She hated him at that moment, almost as much as she feared him. Tears were stinging at the back of Frances's eyes but she would not let him see them fall. She could hardly bear the pain in Josie's sobs, and begged God to make her father leave so that she and Mama could finally run upstairs.

No one dared go up to Josie until Domenic finally went to bed. Frances broke into sobs when she saw how badly Josie was beaten. She looked as if she'd fallen in the path of a runaway horse and buggy.

"Mama," Josie sobbed, collapsing against her mother's chest. "Mama, he made a mess of me."

The next night, when her husband returned from work, Concetta begged him to unchain Josie so that she could relieve herself without using a pan. He didn't say a word when he returned from the girls' bedroom, rehung the dog chain on the hook next to the back door, and sat down for dinner. When Concetta called Josie to join the family and eat something, he sent the plates and silverware rattling with a fist slammed on the table.

"That *puttana* is not leaving her room."

For the duration of the week, Josie was kept prisoner in her room, except for the few hours when Domenic and the older boys were at work. She wept, her mother wept, her sisters and even her little brothers wept, more from confusion than from comprehension of the predicament.

The following Sunday, while Domenic was once again salting the entire plate of food that Concetta had to share, there came a knock on the front door. Domenic left his dinner table to find Nino and a man he instantly recognized standing on his porch in their Sunday best. The man, Nino's neighbor, a powerful Mafioso who had not been able to recruit the young bricklayer, spoke first.

"Excuse me for disturbing your dinner, Signore Costa. Signore Mazzarino, here, has come to see me with his problem. I understand he and your daughter, these young people, have been engaged nearly a year, and that now you have said to them that the wedding is off. Tell me, Signore Costa, is it true you have broken the engagement?"

Domenic pulled himself up and glared first at Nino and then at the man. *He* was the *consigliere*. So what if this big Mafioso was standing on his porch and staring him down, thinking he could walk up his stairs to settle this business.

"This wedding is over. Finished. My daughter is not going to marry this, this . . ."

"Signore Costa," the Mafioso cut him short. "And what does your daughter say?"

"Say? She doesn't have anything to say."

The Mafioso thought otherwise. "I will talk to your daughter."

From the upstairs bedroom to which she'd been banished, Josie was listening. At the Mafioso's words, she was down the stairs and beside her father at the front door before Domenic could formulate a reply. Her curly-haired Nino was at stake and she was ready to gamble with every prayer she possessed. She saw pain flicker through Nino's eyes when he saw her face and arms stained with bruises. But the sight of him, standing against her father with the big Mafioso in his fine hat and striped suit, bolstered her with a courage she didn't know she had.

The Mafioso turned to Josie. "My daughter, I understand you and Signore Mazzarino are engaged nearly one year already to be married. And I understand that your father says that this engagement is broken. What do you say?"

"*He* said it, signore. Not me."

The Mafioso turned to Domenic and said two things.

"Signore Costa, these children are going to be married. And I suggest you make the wedding right away."

Domenic felt a sheen blossom across his forehead in the same instant he understood that he'd wear more than bruises if he refused to comply.

His protest that Josie had not yet completed her trousseau fell on deaf ears.

Gifts for the young couple began to arrive almost immediately, and Concetta and her *cummaris* plied their needles by dim light long into the night to ready all the party dresses. Domenic and Concetta had no money to pay for a wedding feast, so Nino bought the food himself, cheese and eggs and produce and one hundred pounds of almonds and of walnuts, too. The Costa boys hoisted cases of beer down into the cellar and stacked them to chill, the *cummaris* set to baking anise biscotti and fig-filled *cassateddi*, and early in the morning, two days before the wedding, Nino plunked down the cash at Eastern Market, slung a two-hundred-pound side of beef across his shoulders, and to the clop-clop of horses' hooves and the squeal of automobile brakes, he walked it to his bride's home so the women could start simmering it.

Josie and Concetta unpacked the sheets, pillowcases, towels, nightgowns, and bed jackets from Josie's *cassete* and adorned the living room with her needlework for everyone to fuss over. When they weren't cooking, the women of the neighborhood were running in and out of the Costa home, emptying their own cupboards of dishes, glasses, serving bowls, and silverware so the hundred invited guests could eat.

The night before the wedding, Rocco, Pasquale, and Angelo tried one last time to cajole Nino into going to the whorehouse with them, so he'd know what to do with their sister when they got home from their party. Nino reddened and told them he would manage just fine.

Early on the morning of the nuptials, Concetta and her best friend, who stood in Nino's mother's stead, took the wedding sheets to Nino's house and prepared the wedding bed. By the time they returned, the florist was delivering Josie's huge bouquet of daisy mums and ferns and Frances was helping her older sister lace up her high white boots. When the bride was ready, Concetta pulled Frances's long brown hair off her face and tied it with a huge floppy white bow that matched the others she had made for Aggie and Mary.

Then, in procession, the Costa family and their friends walked Josie to the elaborately appointed church, the same way Nino's friends accompanied him. With one hand, he fingered the piece of iron in his pocket, which he put there to ward off *malocchio*, the evil eye. With the other, he formed the *mano cornuto*—horned hand—behind his back. Making a fist, he used his thumb to hold down his two middle fingers, and jutted his extended pointer and pinky in several directions to ward off any instances of *malocchio* the iron failed to divert. At the church, Domenic kissed his daughter on the forehead and welcomed Nino into the family.

Josie and her curly-haired husband exchanged simple gold bands during the wedding Mass, and then everyone hurried to the Costas' backyard to celebrate. It was mid-September and the weather was perfect for an outdoor party, and the *vino* and the music and the food didn't stop for two days. There was soup with chicken and carrots and tiny meatballs, pasta with meat sauce, salads, potatoes, olives, cheeses, roasted beef and chicken, bread, cake, cookies, nuts and fruit, and plenty of strong coffee. Josie and Nino posed for a formal portrait with Frances and Mary, who were their attendants. They laughed and danced the tarantella and brought a dish of cookies to the Mafioso who had changed their fate.

There was a young man at Josie's wedding who did not escape Frances's notice, a young and handsome boy who wanted to be a barber, like his father. He, too, noticed the bride's younger sister, an exceptionally pretty girl with a full lower lip and huge round eyes.

Early the next morning, Concetta and her *cummari* hurried to Nino's house to strip the wedding linens from his bed before Sunday Mass. Afterward, the wedding guests would return to continue the celebration. Proudly, they hung the bloodstained bottom sheet across the curtain rod in the Costas' living room to prove to the community that Domenic's son-in-law had married a virgin.

The wedding excitement died down, and life went on for Frances much as she had imagined it. There was more room in the bed she shared with Aggie and Mary, there was more work to do in the house, and, while she enjoyed the time she had alone with her mother while her siblings were at school, she missed Josie terribly and could not wait from Sunday dinner to Sunday dinner to see her sister again.

True to her fears, while her older brothers mouthed off to their mother about meals or laundry, Frances absorbed the brunt of their opprobrious behavior if her washing and ironing fell short of their exacting standards. One afternoon, when she was watching Luigi do his schoolwork, Rocco came raging at her over a small crease ironed into his shirt.

"You expect me to wear this?" He shoved the shirt toward her face and she began to stammer a reply.

"Shut your face and go do it right this time," Rocco yelled, and kicked Frances for emphasis.

Luigi toppled his chair as he jumped from it to kick Rocco in the shins. Frances was his sweetest sister and his brother was a rotten pig. But before Concetta could reach the dining room to intervene, her eight-year-old son had won himself a welt across his face for defending his sister.

Chapter Fourteen ❧

Corleone, 1912

Garibaldi's Risorgimento had promised much to peasants like my great-grandparents. Italy's boot had been a jigsaw puzzle of feudal city-states, each with its own foreign allegiance and language or dialect, a number of which pledged fealty to the pope. But in the half century that had come and gone since Garibaldi's dream of uniting the Italian peninsula and Sicily into one country was realized, life for the *contadini* had grown even less bearable. No matter how many men and boys in a family rose before dawn to start work, no matter whether their women took in laundry or stitching to supplement their wages, almost all the money they managed to scrape together was needed to purchase meager amounts of food. While compulsory education did little to affect the peasants' lives, compulsory conscription did, yanking needed breadwinners from the home for seven-year stretches. For most, military service was their first venture away from home and their first chance at literacy. For many, it was the stepping-stone to further travels. After seven years in the military, they could sacrifice one or two years to hard labor in America if it enabled them to feed their families. The land they were born on couldn't afford them that same chance.

While the exodus from Italy and Sicily had begun soon after unification failed to put food in the peasants' bellies, it surged after the turn of the twentieth century. In the first decade alone,

more than five million men and boys left their homeland to emi-
grate to Australia and the Americas, North and South, to find
work. In Sicily, four men out of every ten kissed their families
good-bye and headed to Napoli to make the dreaded two-week
ocean crossing crammed inside the belly of a ship. They didn't
leave with the intention of abandoning their homeland. Desperate, starving, they simply saw no choice but to work across the
ocean for a year or two, send their earnings home, and then return
to their loved ones.

Often the family reunion was only long enough to reacquaint a
father with his children before he was forced to turn around and
head to sea again. Some Italians made several Atlantic crossings a
year, working summers in America and returning to their families
each winter. Steamship booking agents dubbed these laborers
"birds of passage," comparing them to migratory birds.

While Concetta still refused to acknowledge her sister Rosalia,
Domenico had always remained in contact with the sister-in-law
he'd deflowered in that crowded Palermo hotel room, and later
with the man she'd eventually married, Matteo Giacobelli. With a
handshake and good wishes, Domenico bid Matteo good-bye
when the young father decided to leave Rosalia and their small
children behind and join up with several others who were leaving
Partinico to go build railroads in a place called Detroit. Domenico
hungered for every shred of news about his friend's adventure.

The work was hard, Matteo reported in letters Rosalia had to
ask someone to read to her, but it was as steady as the pay that regularly made its way into his wife's hands. Matteo said there were
many miles of railroad tracks to be built in America, providing
plentiful jobs with the pick and shovel for starving Italians. The
work was surprisingly familiar. Like farming, it was outside, in the
fresh air. Instead of digging furrows, you dug trenches. Instead of
sowing seeds, you planted railroad tracks. But unlike the seedlings
that stretched upward toward the sun, the metal tracks you put

into the ground stretched in a horizontal line for as far as the eye could see. America had gone rail crazy, just like Northern Italy. But in America, at least, Southern Italians could find jobs. With a strong back and no fear of long days at hard labor, you could find all the work you needed building streetcar rail lines or laying railroad tracks for big steam locomotives.

By early 1912, my great-grandfather Domenico had reached a crossroads. After he'd put in a year or so traveling up and down the countryside selling sacks of farina and testing wine quality, Domenico had packed it in to try his hand at other sales jobs in the hopes that they would prove more lucrative. First he sold hay, then he dabbled briefly in real estate, but what peasant had any money for new housing? Instead of being able to purchase a new home for sons who were marrying, fathers were making room for their daughters-in-law in their own crowded homes.

Domenico moved on to selling insurance, an occupation his American great-grandchildren would one day write with quotation marks that hinted at their suspicions of an involvement with the Corleone Mafiosi that extended beyond his *cumpari* relationship with Salvatore's godfather. Still, Domenico couldn't earn enough to support his family, even with the additional odd money he continued to win in the dance contests. Concetta was an accomplished seamstress, and she could augment their meager income by constructing men's suits, but only when the peasants had money to afford the fabric.

In the meantime, their brother-in-law through marriage, Matteo, had decided not to make the return trip he had planned. He sent Rosalia a letter instructing her to pack up the children and their best belongings and to use the money he'd enclosed to buy them all steerage passage to Detroit. He had no idea it was the nineteenth largest city in America, or that within twenty years it would grow to claim fourth place. All he knew was that he was making money, he was living near other Italians, and his belly was filled with more than just a hunk of bread and an onion. *Ciao, Sicilia.* He was staying in America. So were many others. Six months after Rosalia sailed from Naples, Domenico's own brother, Mario, came to the same conclusion. He tried to convince Domenico to come with him to Detroit, just as the two had moved their families together from Partinico, but at forty-two, Domenico was not easily swayed. He convinced himself to hang on; the insurance business had to improve.

Yet he could see that the families whose men were working across the ocean were faring better than their neighbors. When the "birds of passage" did return to Corleone or Partinico, spiffed up in decent suits of clothing and sporting shoes made of fine polished leather, Domenico took notice. Everyone did. With food in their bellies, smiles on their faces, and a few coins—and sometimes watches—jangling in their pockets, these men with the luster of l'America about them even seemed to walk taller.

"Toil, toil, if you wish to prosper," promised a Sicilian proverb. "Heaven rains water and hail, not money." But for those who toiled in Sicily, another proverb proved more true. "With honest toil you never get there, and the effort hardly sustains you."

"If you won't go, then I am going to America," Rocco told his father. He repeated it so often and with such increasing determination that Concetta became fearful. "Domenico, go," she pleaded. "If Rocco goes to l'America on his own, we will never see him again."

Still, Domenico was torn. Yes, life was hard for peasants like the Costas, but it had its familiar patterns and rhythms. On Sundays, no one missed Mass, everyone said an extra rosary, and he was one of the men who thronged the barbershop from dawn until the middle of the afternoon to indulge in their weekly need for a shave and gossip. On summer nights, after they had thanked God for their dinner, praised the Madonna, and remembered their dead, his family and their neighbors' families moved outside to sit and joke and visit as a community. They congregated outside one home or another, and the women kept at their weaving until dusk, while the adults shared stories and jokes and interjected opinions on everything, usually unasked. Sometimes the children played, but mostly they sat and listened, knowing better than to mix in.

In winter the evening ritual moved indoors. Families clustered around the large brazier in the large room, warming their toes beneath its round brass tray aglow with coals perfumed with dried citrus peels. The children sat wide-eyed while the mamas and *nonnas* regaled them with the most fantastical tales.

Each night, his children ran to him and Concetta for a bedtime blessing when Domenico decreed, as the papas always did, that now everyone needed to go off to sleep.

On New Year's Day, the Costas didn't dare eat macaroni for fear of having misery and hardship throughout the year—for whatever you did on New Year's Day, you'd surely do all year. Instead, as even the poorest Sicilians managed to do, they feasted on wine and *lasagne cacate*—"shitty noodles." These special noodles were wide and curly, bought from the baker and tossed with ricotta cheese and sauce at the New Year dinner table. Early on Ascension Day, Domenico and his family washed their faces in the morning dew to ward off skin disorders and then they drank the dew, mixed with water, believing that it would impart strength and protection from illness.

On the one hand there was custom, tradition, and what their descendants would call superstition. On the other there was abject poverty—and the latter was becoming more familiar to Domenico than anything else.

Finally, he came to his decision. Once he could manage to eke out enough money for passage to Detroit, he was going.

He decided to make this first trip across the ocean alone. Although Rocco was anxious to accompany him, he would leave his eldest sons in Corleone for now. At seventeen, fourteen, and thirteen, Rocco, Pasquale, and Angelo could go out each morning with the laborers who congregated before dawn in the town square, hoping to be hired out for one day, two, or more. That way, when they got lucky, a little local money might still make its way into the house. From his previous extended absences while off peddling flour, Domenico was confident that, as the eldest, Rocco could see to the household matters and could well supervise his mother and sisters in his father's stead.

Giuseppina and Francesca were daunted by the news of their father's plan. L'America was so far away, a ship took two entire weeks to get there! They feared they would never see him again. From past experience, they also knew how firmly their older brothers flexed their power when they were left in command.

Huddled with Agata and Maria in the tiny bed they shared, every night the small sisters whispered fervent prayers that they'd awaken in the morning to hear that their father had changed his mind. When morning came and their petitions went unanswered, the girls turned to prayers that a toad would hop into their house on the following Friday, certain it would actually be a Lady of the Outside come to keep their father in Corleone. From early childhood, every peasant knew to treat a toad with only kindness and respect. If one hopped inside the house, the entire family would lavish it with attention and tidbits of food. They were afraid not to. For any toad might actually be one of the Ladies of the Outside, fabled fairies who possessed the power to make peasants rich, but who also would exact merciless revenge if they were injured or offended. Elegant and ephemeral beings all week long, these Ladies were bound to earth by a curse that transformed them into ugly toads on Fridays.

My great-grandmother Concetta understood her little ones' apprehension about their father's decision to leave for America. She was conflicted as well. Yes, she was used to his absence from the home and to his marital wanderings, but Detroit was a long way to wander, and now Rosalia was living there. Concetta had also observed how other Corleonesi women struggled to keep their households in order while their husbands were away for extended periods. Even with the security of having older sons still in the home, it was not easy for a Sicilian woman to be without her man. More than ever, Concetta would become a prisoner in her own home. Yet undeniably, she and Domenico had eleven mouths to feed, and just as undeniably, crossing the Atlantic was Domenico's only chance now at sustaining them all.

By the first of May, a bright maze of flowers spilled across Sicily's hillsides, dipping and waving on the breeze as if bowing a welcome to spring's newest and most special flower, the yellow daisy. *Ciuri di maju,* the Sicilians named them—flowers of May—were feted annually with a woman's holiday.

Sometime during the night in which April morphed into May, Francesca's eyes popped open with anticipation and refused to close again. Unable to sleep, she lay in bed struggling to control her excitement. How many hours until Mama called them to run out to pick daisies? She could almost hear the chatter and laughter of the mothers and daughters who would soon be descending on the hills to celebrate the ancient annual ritual. Throughout Sicily, every female who could walk would scurry from home at daybreak to greet the month considered most auspicious for love and new beginnings. Finally, she poked her sisters awake, hurrying them to get dressed. The four girls sat at the edge of the loft, swinging their feet as if they could help shoo the cloak of night from the sky. The minute Concetta poked her head from the shadows of her bedroom, the girls clambered down the ladder and were out the door.

Laughter echoed through the countryside as the young girls plucked up daisies to tuck into their hair and bodices while their mothers, aunts, and grandmothers collected blossoms they bunched into bouquets. Extending an arm toward the nearest church, the women offered their daisies to God and prayed for a year of good fortune. "O Divine Protector, provide for me. Divine Providence, comfort me. Divine Providence, so very great, whoever has faith in God never will perish." As they scattered each bunch of daisies and bent to pick more, the women kept at their prayers.

"I see May, and I gather May. I want no woes in my home. Flowers of May, I pick in the fields. Gold and silver in my pockets!" The women chanted the familiar prayers to bring prosperity to the home and to dispatch woes and bed bugs from it, as they stuffed the golden blossoms into their pockets and pretended they were coins. Their lips moved with other prayers, too, composed on the spot and filled with personal petitions. Some begged success for their spouses in America, others prayed their men would find work at home. This May, Concetta's prayers for the year were especially devout.

Her daughters frolicked nearby with other girls their age, running to her now and again with their stubby-stemmed offerings. As Giuseppina watched the older girls gather in a circle to talk of romance, she informed her sisters that she intended to marry a man with curly hair. Francesca wandered closer to the big girls, who had settled on the grass, giggling and laughing. Wistfully she dreamed of a time when she, too, would be old enough to think about marriage. Then she and Giuseppina, possibly Agata, too, would be sitting in just such a circle pulling petals one by one, their hearts beating with an anxious thrill as they raced to discover with the final petal whether their *fidanzato* loved them or not.

She knew that Flora, who was not engaged but who had designs on Carlo, was asking the petals if she would become his *fidanzata* this year. And everyone knew that Pia, who had been engaged for four years, was praying for her father to return from America, finally, with a proper dowry so that she could marry her Vincenzo. Like the older girls Francesca studied, who tossed down one denuded stem and picked up a fresh one, she knew that if she and her sisters didn't like the petals' first answer, they could just ask another daisy to tell their future, and another.

Within a few hours, Concetta and her four daughters had stuffed enough golden daisies into their aprons to bring a year's worth of prosperity into their tiny home. Little fingers helped tie together bunches of the golden blossoms to hang on the walls and on their looms, and helped weave two fine necklaces of daisies, one to festoon their donkey and another one to bring luck to their dog, Bruna. Cheeks flushed with sunshine and laughter, the girls ran into the house and spilled out their daisies across the floor. They spent the rest of the afternoon helping their mother assemble daisies to toss in the pantry and underneath their beds, and when they had decorated the entire household with gold, they brought the rest outside to spread around their brothers' farming tools.

The first of May was also a day devoted to prayers to Saint James and Saint Philip, venerated as the devil's most pertinacious foes. And on this date more than any other, Sicilians knew for certain that all the devils were in the air.

"No one touches the flour today." Concetta slapped Francesca's hand away from the sack of farina, as her girls began tucking their daisies into the pantry. "Sift flour today and you stir up devils and flour roaches, and in this house we don't want either one. Quick now, everyone say the prayer."

With a little shiver, the older girls began the powerful incantation, convinced it would scare away any devils they might have inadvertently stirred up. "Blessed Saint Philip and Saint James, powerful appointed apostles, Agnus Dei, Agnus Dei, Agnus Dei, bless and clear the air!" Concetta and her daughters quickly made the sign of the cross, but their prayer was not finished. Even the little ones piped up then, scrunching their chubby cheeks as they raised their voices at the devil. "Out, ugly beast!"

During the last week of May, Domenico shoved his dancing pallet beneath the bed, disturbing the slumber of the lucky daisies drying there. Grabbing his few changes of clothing, he stuffed them into a traveling sack Concetta had sewed for his journey. Even as they watched him add a cup, a bowl, and some eating utensils to his sack, Giuseppina, Francesca, Agata, and Maria kept up their silent prayers that somehow he would change his mind.

Then, with a formal good-bye and *lire* equivalent to twenty-five dollars in his pocket, Domenico left Rocco in charge of the family and of his wife's and his daughters' honor. His words were slow, deliberate, a caveat to the assembled family.

"Besides health, honor is our biggest prize on this earth. Honor is the spirit of God shining on our face. It is a man's duty to avenge offended honor, commanded by God himself. Remember this. Its stain cannot be washed away by any judge. A man can only wash it away with blood."

Domenico hefted up his satchel and reminded his younger sons that they were free to offer Rocco their opinions and advice during the seven months he planned to be away. "But until I am back in this house, Rocco's word is the law. *Capiddu?*"

And then my great-grandfather walked through the door without kissing my great-grandmother good-bye, for displays of affection in front of the children or in a public arena were rare. It would take him several days to reach the port in Palermo, and he had tacked on some additional travel time. He had a number of good-byes to take care of along the way.

The ocean voyage proved as hideous as he had been warned it would be. After suffering through thirteen days of seasickness, not all of it his own, Domenico disembarked and filled his lungs with the warm June air. Although they had been cleared by doctors at the port in Palermo, he and the other passengers still had to clear the numerous examinations at Ellis Island. For nearly half the day he was shuttled from doctors to inspectors to intake officials, every one of them jabbering at him in a language he would not have understood if not for the interpreters shadowing them. They checked his eyes, they examined his head, they rattled off countless questions, and they passed him down the line until finally, unbelieving, Domenico was standing wide-eyed in the streets of New York. Swallowed up in the chaotic crowd of newly landed immi-

grants and the relatives awaiting them, he shouldered his way in
the direction of the waiting taxicabs, scanning the throng for the
first glimpse in nearly two years of his brother, Mario.

He doubted he could fall asleep tonight, despite the long train
ride to Detroit. Tomorrow they would drink to his arrival with
their Sicilian *cumparis* in a house whose address he had seen
scrawled across the back of each of Mario's letters to Corleone. A
two-story house, built out of wood, on Rivard Street in Detroit,
Michigan, the United States of America. Tomorrow night he
would fall asleep there, and the following morning, Domenico was
certain, he would find himself a job.

Chapter Fifteen ❧

Corleone, 1913

My great-grandfather didn't make it back to Corleone for more than a year. He returned bearing an envelope filled with some cash and three steamship tickets, steerage, back to America—one for himself, one for Rocco, and one for Pasquale. He was taking them to Detroit to work for Henry Ford. He'd begun saving for their passage at the beginning of the year, on the day that Ford announced he was raising his workers' pay to five dollars a day and cutting their workday from nine hours to eight. The sum was dizzying to Domenico. It was craziness. It was double the salary Ford's competitors General Motors and Chrysler paid their employees, and much more than he earned on the railroad.

But Mr. Ford wasn't done. In addition, he declared, he was going to pay his male workers a portion of his company's profits. Men had stampeded that January morning to apply, nearly twelve thousand of them causing near riots at Ford's gates before firemen called to the factory finally turned their hoses on them. Even though all of l'America had only ten miles of paved road, this motorcar business of Mr. Ford's was growing. Was Domenico going to be a fool and leave his eldest sons in Corleone now? Talk of war was already brewing. They were better off away from Sicily and with him. Let it be Angelo's turn to guard the family honor. Even if Rocco and Pasquale had to swing a hammer alongside him on the railroad for a few months at first, Domenico was going to get his family working for Mr. Henry Ford.

Domenico had more far-reaching plans brewing, but he didn't confide them to Concetta or to his sons. In six or seven months, he calculated, he and his boys should earn enough money laying railroad track to bring all eleven Costas to America. They'd save even more by sleeping in railroad cars instead of renting a room. And if even one of the three was lucky enough to land a job at Mr. Ford's automobile factory, it could all happen sooner.

The more Rocco and Pasquale listened to their father's stories about America, the more they itched to leave, grumbling that his two-week visit home was too long. They were restless to leave for Palermo, eager to see the grand lights of New York. Domenico told anybody who would listen that he liked it in Detroit. He liked the way he was able to live there. He liked America and its promises of a New Freedom, the campaign platform on which Woodrow Wilson had just ridden his way to the White House. Sure, President Wilson had also brought with him America's first personal income tax law, but Domenico wasn't complaining. That tax was still less than the money he and his sons had been forced to pay to the landowners, and less than the *posas* that had been levied on him by the mill owners.

Francesca sat at her father's feet and looked at him as if he was concocting fairy tales when he told his family about the first assembly line, which Henry Ford had just invented for his factory in Highland Park, outside Detroit. "No, Francesca, this is all true," he told her, describing how a conveyor belt brought partially assembled automobiles to the various workers. "I, myself, know other *Siciliani* who work there who have seen this with their own eyes. A car that used to take them twelve hours to put together? Now they can make one in just ninety-three minutes! Thousands a year they can make this way." Francesca could barely imagine one automobile. She had no conception of what a thousand of them might be.

Seen through her father's eyes, Detroit was bustling, exciting, modern, unfathomable—truly a magical place. It was called the most American of cities, he told them, even though one out of every three men there was born in a foreign country. There were lots of Italians there, and three Italian theaters, with stars from New York and Rome. There was something called an amusement park, sparkling with lights and filled with machines that spun people in the air and sent them barreling up and down steep hills built out of metal.

"Detroit is our future," Papa told her brothers. "In Detroit, we can earn for our families, provide—not sweat under the thumb of the landowners. In Detroit, we can be men." Francesca measured the change in her father, the energy he exuded when he spoke about Detroit, the sparkle in his eyes that she had never seen before. He even walked differently. Like other "birds of passage," her father did not return still dressed in the mantle of defeat. Detroit was their future, Papa said. Sicily was their past.

Angelo was never as cruel a taskmaster as Rocco had been, but Concetta noticed that he'd absorbed some of his eldest brother's roughness. He rose each morning to join the others looking for day work, but more and more Angelo would be out at night, running with a group in the countryside.

The Costas' bedtime prayer routine had changed when Domenico left, and changed again when Rocco and Pasquale went to America with him. After their usual evening prayers were said, Concetta led the children in additional prayers for their father's and brothers' safety, and they thanked God and the Virgin Mother for the extra money coming to them from across the ocean. Now, while Concetta lay awake listening for Angelo to return home, she prayed for him, too. When Concetta or one of the children awakened in the night to hear Angelo creeping from the house, they worried that he might be involved with one of the groups who ran the countryside under the cover of night. Concetta didn't know which of the scenarios she feared frightened her more—that Angelo ran with the brigand "Robin Hoods" who took matters into their own hands to right injustices they saw occurring among the *contadini*. Or that he was involved with the gang of *contadini* toughs who hired themselves out to the landowners' *gabellotti* as armed retainers, protecting their farms from cattle rustlers and looters. Either way, with justice more and more often being meted out man-to-man, come daylight husbands and sons you'd least expect were turning up sprawled on parched back roads newly watered with their blood.

Three weeks after her husband and sons departed for America, Concetta's breasts began to swell with a familiar tenderness. Two months later, her belly began to balloon as well. Four months later, a letter arrived from Domenico, which Angelo read aloud to the family at supper.

"Wife, sell the house and the furniture for the best price you can, and pack up the necessities. In March, I return to Corleone to bring you and the children. There is nothing more for us in Sicilia. It is time you come live here with us in Detroit."

Angelo tossed the letter into the air with a whoop and his siblings began to scream and laugh and jump around with such excitement, the neighbors came running from their own table to see what had triggered so much commotion in the Costa home.

"L'America! Papa is coming back and taking us to l'America!"

It was all Concetta could think about, talk about, smile about in the weeks that followed.

With the help of a male cousin who had worked in real estate, she established prices and secured buyers for the Costas' dwelling and their largest furnishings. What she couldn't sell and couldn't take, she distributed to relatives and friends. Bit by bit, she dismantled her household and began to pack the remnants of her family's former life inside a large wooden trunk destined for Detroit.

The change in the Costa family, even down to the baby, Salvatore, was evident to everyone. With one letter, they had become animated and happy. With that letter, they'd been given hope. A future. So elated was she about relocating to America, Concetta didn't even permit the eventuality of a long sea voyage during her eighth month of pregnancy to daunt her. Every kick of her baby in utero reminded her that those little feet were not going to learn to walk on Sicilian soil.

"This baby will be born a *'Medicano*," she crowed to the other women also filling their jugs from the fountain in the piazza.

"Oh, the little *'Medicano* is restless today," she chuckled, rubbing her belly with a small smile while sewing with the neighbor women outside their houses. Bent over her needle, she was oblivious of the glances that passed around her.

"Ah, my little *'Medicano*," she crooned, her voice lilting so that the nearby female acquaintances could hear, "your mama is going to have to find you a proper *'Medicano* name."

"You know, Concetta, you've got a big mouth," one of the neighbor women finally called out.

In a flash, Concetta was off her stool and in the woman's face. Before anyone could stop her, she jammed her index fingers inside the corners of the woman's mouth and ripped sideways, splitting open her friend's lips.

"Really?" Concetta asked, with a dip of her head toward the woman, who sat stunned and bleeding, fingers clutched to her lips. Concetta looked with satisfaction at the drops of blood decorating her friend's needlework. "So now who's got the big mouth?"

Chapter Sixteen ❧

Detroit, 1917

If the Costa boys hadn't maneuvered their way up through the ranks of the gangs they ran with before Prohibition, no doubt they found employment with the Sicilian rumrunners once Detroit went dry.

Seven weeks after Josie and Nino's wedding, Detroiters helped vote in statewide prohibition of the sale of beer, wine, and liquor, effective May 1, 1917. Although the 353,378 to 284,754 vote prohibited only the sale of alcohol, it also ended its manufacture or purchase, because a federal law already on the books prohibited its manufacture and purchase in states that barred its sale. Immediately, Detroiters began stockpiling all the beer, wine, and hard liquor they could get their hands on.

The fifty thousand citizens who swarmed to hear baseball player turned electrifying evangelist Billy Sunday preach his fall-long "Detroit Crusade" may have tipped the vote, but teetotaling was no new concept to Michiganders. Their State Fair had been dry since 1911, and their counties had been exercising the right to opt free of alcohol since the late 1880s. By 1916, forty-five of its eighty-three counties had already adopted dry ordinances. Nationwide, voters were doing the same.

From the coal fields and into the cities, temperance workers had been marching across the country preaching the evils of alcohol. Before her death in 1911, six-foot-tall, one-hundred-seventy-five-pound Carry Nation had wielded her hatchet across a number of states, smashing up saloons and convincing voters that alcohol destroyed families. Taking up Nation's campaign for a better life for their children and themselves, American women beat the bandwagon for prohibition. Pledging that "lips that touch liquor will never touch mine," they swayed their menfolk—the only ones who were enfranchised at the time—to leave their saloons and vote for abstinence. By 1913, more than half the U.S. population was living under prohibition.

Michigan became the test case for federally mandated Prohibition, and then the nation's test case for Prohibition enforcement. Although Ontario, Canada, was also dry territory, the manufacture of alcoholic beverages destined for "wet" counties was still legal in Ontario. Detroiters could see the crates of booze piled on the shipping docks that stretched the length of Windsor's shoreline, barely one mile across the Detroit River. Most of that booze never reached its purported destination, but ended up in dry counties instead.

Immigrant men like Domenic Costa, who were not citizens and had no say in deciding Michigan's Prohibition, were flabbergasted that the voters had outlawed alcohol. These were men? What kind of men let their women bully them into sobriety? Or nodded their heads in support of these *pazzi* ("crazy") *'Medicani* females who were also screaming for their right to suffrage? Even the cowboys in Montana put down their lassos to vote the first woman ever into the United States House of Representatives, Jeannette Rankin, a college-educated woman who espoused women's rights. Well, it was Domenic's right to have a glass of *vino* with his dinner or his lunch, or his breakfast if he wanted to, no matter what Mr. Ford and these crazy *'Medicani* had to say about it.

Domenic soon discovered that no one was paying much attention to the law. The word in Detroit was that if you couldn't find a drink, you just weren't trying. Bootleggers could shoot their speed-boats across the Detroit River in four minutes flat, and in the winter, they'd drive doorless cars across the ice—easier to load up—and drive back. Alcohol smuggling became a part-time, small-scale occupation for ordinary citizens. Everyone was carry-ing contraband booze from Canada or neighboring Ohio, even women and children, who slipped bottles into the long narrow pockets of the ingeniously designed vests and underskirts they wore beneath their clothing. Mechanics refitted cars with false bottoms and yanked out fuel tanks to replace them with dual com-partments to hold both fuel and booze. Undertakers drove hearses carrying caskets crammed with liquor. And Detroiters went on en-joying their cocktails at home and in their restaurants as if Prohi-bition had never been passed. Dixie Highway, in both directions, was clogged with cars from Detroit to Toledo, Ohio, which was "wet." The cops couldn't stop them all if they'd wanted to. Enter-prising individuals hid stills in their basements, bought ingredi-ents at the dime store, and brewed homemade "tarantula juice," which they sold for fifteen bucks a gallon. The Sicilians dubbed the one-hundred-ninety-proof stuff "tarantella juice" instead, a pun on their lively folk dance.

Domenic was scheming as well. He knew something about wine. Hadn't his evaluation set the price the French buyers paid for the white wine of his region?

Suddenly, no one in his household was able to take more than a sponge bath. He commandeered the family bathtub, stopped it up, and filled it with the wine he started making in the basement. He hauled home cases of red grapes from Eastern Market, which fer-mented into a passable red wine that even Domenic drank. His sons helped him fill the bottles, and he taught his daughters to use a special machine to cork them. After dark, the boys took the wine out back to hide it in the garage. Domenic ran a length of pipe from the back porch to the garage so family members could bang a warning to anyone working in the garage.

Domenic also bought for a song the farmers' shriveled spoiled

grapes—the "raisins" they were ready to toss into the garbage—
and made a second, inferior wine. The kind he had no compunction
about bottling up and selling as the good dago stuff to the unsuspecting blacks who lived in neighborhoods adjoining the Sicilian
part of town. He had no qualms about "making *fesso*" of them.

By August 1917, when his certificate of exemption from military
service was issued, Nino had moved his Josie to a house on Chestnut Street. As a resident alien, he would not be called up to serve
in World War I, as many young Detroiters had been since the
United States entered the war in April. Their absence from the
workplace was of such impact that, for the first time, women had
begun taking over their men's jobs. Nearly two hundred thousand
Detroit women registered for war work, stepping into jobs as mail
carriers and streetcar conductors. The ethnic women, however, remained at home, cooking and cleaning and raising their children.
Josie made Nino's bed and Nino's pasta and waited for the day
when she could finally tell him she was making his baby, too. She
had already stood as *cummari* at the baptism of a friend's first
baby, and she couldn't wait to cuddle one of her own.

From the time Frances turned fourteen in early October, Domenic
was needling Concetta to begin considering a match for her.
Frances was stunning, the kind of young woman men took notice
of. By her age, he said, Josie had been engaged. Concetta had a
hunch that Frances had already set her heart on the young barber,
Giuseppe Falco. She observed the way Frances sneaked glances at
him from beneath lowered lashes when he walked past their pew
to take communion, how her cheeks flushed whenever he met her
glance as they left or entered the church. Recently she had observed the two young people speaking to each other on the church
steps after Mass, innocently enough, publicly enough that Domenic
didn't stop them. They stood the proper few paces apart, Frances

usually with Aggie at her side, and Concetta could see that young Giuseppe was smiling and animated when he talked with her daughter.

He was from a good family, although she hadn't spoken with his mother more than to exchange greetings with her at church. His father owned the barbershop not far from them where her older sons often went for a haircut and shave. Giuseppe was just a year older than Frances, but he already had a steady job in his father's business. Since even Josie had made a comment to her about the way Frances's demeanor changed whenever she was within a few feet of Giuseppe, Concetta decided it was time to make a few more inquiries about the young barber. Then she would have a talk with Frances and proceed from there. The girl had been diligent about working on her trousseau, so that was nearly finished. And Josie's wedding dress was waiting for her in the bottom drawer of Concetta's dresser. It would take no time to run a new seam up the sides to accentuate Frances's trimmer figure.

Domenic, meantime, was beginning to hatch his own plan about a match for his second daughter. Rumrunning was getting to be a bigger enterprise than just the part-time exploit of individual opportunists looking to make an easy buck. As states one by one began to ratify the national Prohibition amendment to the Constitution, Domenic and others like him realized that supplying the country with alcohol was soon going to be big business, and the likely source for that alcohol lay approximately a mile away, in Windsor.

Right now any enterprising individual could clear a seventy-five-dollar profit on each barrel of beer or case of booze he smuggled, fifteen times the maximum wage he could earn at Ford, money he'd have to pay income taxes on to boot. Even after making payoffs to the lookouts and the police, sometimes a bottle or two, sometimes cash, rumrunning brought in damn good money. With Detroit poised to become the funnel through which the country would guzzle its alcohol, organized crime gangs moved swiftly to corner the profits. The Jewish Purple Gang and the Sicilian street gangs began taking their fights outside their own enclaves as each vied to control the lion's share of the liquor traffic crisscrossing the Detroit River.

What did Domenic's sons need with the Ford plant when they could move up in their own Sicilian gangs and reap some of the profits of this crazy American law? His boys were already doing a few jobs here and there, stealing tires, stealing a few automobiles. They just needed to get themselves more noticed, then move up to the more lucrative action, and Domenic had a hunch about a way to maneuver his boys into choice jobs with one particular gang. The son of the capo—the boss—was still unmarried at age thirty-four, and it was practically unheard of for a Sicilian to walk around single nearly seven years past the proper age to take a wife.

By late March, Domenic had gathered up enough moxie to make his move. Before Concetta could find an opportunity to discuss a match between Frances and the young barber with her husband, Domenic brought home four pounds of beef and ordered her to prepare a pan of *braciole,* a dish of rolled steak stuffed with scallion, hardboiled egg, and ham and roasted in a gravy of onion and bay leaf. He told her to set an extra place at Sunday dinner. He had invited an important guest to come to meet Frances.

Before he had even finished sliding his right wheels alongside the curb in front of the Costas' house, half the kids in the neighborhood were streaming from their yards to gape at Calogero Romano's limousine. They barely glanced at the tall well-dressed man who stepped from the long automobile. They were too spellbound by his narrow Type 57 Cadillac Town Limousine, with its high radiator and high, elongated hood. The car had a windshield, but there was nothing but sky above the front seat—the roof was designed to cover only the passengers sitting in the rear of the limo. Whoever this guy was, he had to be rolling in some cash. Only a rich man owned a car he couldn't drive in crummy weather.

Frances had no clue what her father had in mind when he introduced Calogero Romano to his family and handed him the first glass of wine, but by the time she carried the first course from the kitchen, a platter of *pasta con sarde*, a sick feeling was beginning to churn in her stomach.

"My daughter, she knows how to make this dish better than her mother," Domenic said, passing the platter of pasta with sardines, fennel, and raisins to the guest sitting at his right. "And her bread? Here, *mangia!*" Domenic handed over a round of cheese, with a nod to the thick chunk of bread in Calogero's hand. "So light it's going to float off your plate if you don't slap a nice slice of *touma* on it."

And so it began, against Frances's will, the Sunday dinners with Calogero Romano seated to her father's right, the late Sunday afternoons seated in the living room wearing one of her three good dresses, she on one side, Calogero on the other, making awkward small talk across her parents' chairs. Throughout that spring and summer, on Sunday mornings she would exchange furtive glances with Giuseppe in church and a word or two on the steps, if she was lucky. On Sunday nights, her brother later told me, she would cry herself to sleep.

Spring had brought another unwelcome guest to Frances's neighborhood, as a horrific influenza epidemic ravaged the world in 1918, claiming nearly fifty million people, babies and old people and those in between. With Detroit a major center for troop movement to and from the front in Europe, it was among the cities hardest hit. On a single day in March, one thousand Ford workers were sent home from work with the flu.

Summer brought a lull in the virulence of the epidemic, and Detroiters thought the flu had migrated to Europe, where death tolls kept rising. But by fall, the epidemic in the States was again out of control. Josie was inconsolable when her infant godson was buried, and secretly grateful she had borne no babies for death to steal. Detroit police and public workers walked the streets in gauze masks, and so did skittish citizens, who demanded laws against public sneezing, coughing, even nose-blowing. Theaters, churches, and schools closed. As one in four Americans succumbed to the virulent strain of flu, the Costas and other Italians strung garlic necklaces around their necks to ward off germs, and many gargled with bicarbonate of soda, painted their chests with poultices, doused themselves in camphor, or sought escape from death in other types of folk cures.

To her relief, Calogero Romano's visits to Frances came to a halt for much of the fall. Even within extended families, people mingled only when absolutely necessary. When Domenic Costa declared it was not absolutely necessary to go to church, Frances wasn't able to see Giuseppe Falco, either.

The Spanish flu, as it became known, claimed ten times as many Americans as the war did. Fear gripped every block in De troit, as more and more houses sat swathed in mourning bunting, and over four thousand residents fell to the epidemic before it ran its course by late October. Detroiters' relief at their release from death's grip spilled over into jubilation just a few weeks later. On November 11, 1918, they flooded the streets, screaming at the news that the Great War had ended.

Chapter Seventeen ❧

By Thanksgiving the Costas were attending weekly Mass once more and Calogero was again a Sunday fixture in their home. It was evident that he was smitten with Frances.

Her hurried conversations with the barber outside the church may have escaped Domenic's notice, but her older brothers were more observant. Pasquale made an offhand comment to Calogero one Sunday as he was getting into his black winter Cadillac. The following week Calogero showed up for Sunday Mass at Holy Family Church instead of worshiping with his family at the San Francesco Church, in the older Italian parish. From that morning, he escorted Frances home from Sunday Mass, walking in the company of her family, making his intentions most public. Frances's Sunday conversations with Giuseppe were over. All she had left were her prayers and furtive glances. And a plan.

Several times a week Frances and her sisters had chores outside the house. Once a week they beat the rugs on the clothesline in the backyard. Several times a week they had laundry to hang. Come summertime, there would be tomatoes and peppers to pick, or mint to snip from along the back fence near the alley. Frances wrote a note to Giuseppe, which Aggie slipped to him from her glove the following Sunday after Mass. If he could get away from the barbershop for a few minutes once a week, Frances wrote, she could sneak down to the fence along the alley and they could talk. He sent a message back to her through Aggie a week later, and signed it "Joe."

And so Frances's secret romance with her barber began. Once or twice a week he tromped through the snowy alley to court her with stolen snatches of conversation whispered across the back fence. Busying themselves with their chores nearer to the back porch, her younger sisters stood on the lookout. And week after week, every Sunday that winter, Frances sat dutiful and miserable in the living room, making minimal conversation with a man old enough to be her father. She opened his Christmas present, relieved to find it was a pearl rosary and not a ring. While she gave him no encouragement, Frances was not rude to Calogero. Trapped though she was, she wouldn't behave in a manner to dishonor her father or her family. Under her papa's glare, she stared past Calogero to the falling snow and then to the spring raindrops dotting the front window. She nodded politely, thinking back to Josie's courtship with Nino and imagining it was Joe Falco sitting across from her instead.

"Mama, why is Papa doing this to me? I will die if he makes me marry that old man!"

Concetta knew that Frances was repulsed by Calogero, but she also knew he would provide well for her, and that it was pointless to challenge Domenico.

"Don't you disrespect your father," she warned Frances. "Do you hear?"

Lent began. Frances despaired. At any moment, Calogero could ask for her hand, and a man like Calogero Romano would not wait another year to marry. Her father would readily agree to the *conuscenza*, the engagement. Six months from now, she could turn sixteen as a married woman.

Fearing that his final opportunity at a courtship with Frances would quickly disappear, Joe told her he was going to approach her father. Frances became frantic.

"Calogero will never stand for it. His boys will do something awful to you. No, Joe, please. Not you. Why can't you ask your mother to come to my mother? It's our way. Calogero would never do harm to your mother."

"Frances, your mother will laugh my mother off your porch. Her husband is a *consigliere*. My mother's husband is a barber who pays protection money to Calogero's father so nobody busts up our barbershop. There is no chance."

Again Frances broached the subject with her mother, who still had no inkling of the romance that had braved winter snows and spring gales beside her back gate.

"Are you crazy, Francesca? You prefer to marry a poor barber when you have a rich man who adores you? It's impossible. Your father would never agree."

"But Mama, what if I don't love the rich man who 'adores' me? Is that fair? No one stopped Josie from marrying the man she loves."

Concetta set down her chopping knife and looked at the tears brimming in her daughter's eyes.

"We'll see what we can do, Francesca. Calogero hasn't asked for a *conuscenza* yet. In the meantime, be a good girl and do what your father tells you."

Though Concetta pressed her daughter to show filial obedience, she still went to her husband. But Domenic only laughed and would hear none of it. His life was on the upswing. In fact, he told his wife, he'd just arranged to purchase a horse and a cart.

"I've had enough with the railroad, Concetta. I am going into business for myself. I know a good horse when I see one, and this good horse is going to take me up and down the streets, selling popcorn and ice cream."

His boys' situation was on the upswing, too, he reminded her. Rocco and Pasquale had just completed their first bit of business for Calogero's father, and all had gone well. Everything was going just as he'd planned. There was no need for Giuseppe Falco to come calling on his daughter when he had just promised her to another man.

When Flora di Giovanni Falco knocked on Concetta's door and asked if she had a hen about fifteen years old that might be for sale, Concetta furrowed her eyebrows and shook her head.

"No, my friend, I am quite sorry to disappoint you. The only hens I have for sale are just thirteen and eleven."

The first hint Frances had of her engagement to Calogero came on Easter Sunday when he arrived for dinner with a ring box in his hand. Only the power in her father's blue eyes stopped her from bolting from the room. Her mother and brothers admired the ring, but Frances could not bear to look at the solitaire set in gold, or at her younger sisters, who had suddenly lowered their eyes and gone shy. While everyone saluted the couple with toasts of congratulations and good fortune, she sat at the table with no expression and no appetite, aware of nothing but the weight of Calogero's ring on her hand, because it felt like a manacle. Before the year was up, she would be shackled forever to a man she did not love.

The minute Calogero was gone, Frances ripped the diamond from her finger and fled to her room, sobbing.

"Just take care of the kitchen," Domenic told Concetta when she glanced toward the ceiling with concern. "That girl will come to her senses, even if I have to knock that sense into her."

Two days later, Joe met Frances at the back fence, eyes wide. Was it true? Three months and she would be Romano's wife?

"I won't marry him, Joe. I promise you. I can't."

She wore Calogero's ring only on Sundays, for she dared not defy her father publicly, but in church she hid her left hand in the folds of her skirt to spare her Joe the anguish of seeing another man's ring on her hand.

Three weeks after her engagement, Pasquale mashed his thumb in the assembly line and came home bleeding and early, just in time to see Joe Falco running through the alley. Frances snapped the laundry and tried to breathe normally while she pinned it to the line, but she saw Pasquale squinting at her with harsh eyes and her face flushed red in spite of herself.

"Who were you talking to?" he demanded.

"No one. What do you mean? Blackie." Her words were tumbling too fast. "The only one I was talking to is Blackie. Right, doggie?"

Pasquale came toward his sister and kicked the dog. "That's better, bitch," he hollered after the yelping mutt as it tore for shelter under the back porch. "You gotta answer Frances next time when she talks to you."

Pasquale passed his hunch along to his father and to Calogero, and told his brothers to keep an eye out for anything unusual in the alley. Next time he thought his sister was up to something funny, he wouldn't kick the dog.

For a few weeks, Frances and Joe were afraid to chance a quick encounter more than once a week, usually on the afternoons she was outside beating the rugs. As each visit passed without detection, the two of them lingered a bit longer at the back gate before they could tear themselves away. It was Calogero who spied Joe Falco slipping from the alley one afternoon in mid-June after he'd dropped by the Falcos' shop for a shave and found two Sicilians waiting for old man Falco while his son's barber chair sat empty. That evening, Domenic was startled to find Calogero Romano at his front door, come to pay a call on his future in-laws to request that they put his fiancée on notice. He would tolerate no more backdoor visits from Joe Falco.

Domenic's face blanched white, but rage simmered in his belly even as he swore to Calogero that nothing like this would ever happen again. Pasquale was up the stairs and landing the first blow on his sister before Calogero had stepped off the sidewalk and opened his limo door.

"*Perduno,*" Frances whimpered with each blow, struggling to shield her face with her arms. "I'm sorry, Pasquale."

"The end, you *puttana*! The end of this, do you hear?"

"I'm sorry. I didn't mean it. *Perduno . . .*"

．　．　．

When Calogero arrived at Mass that Sunday, he was horrified by the bruises yellowing on her face and neck. His eyes narrowed on Domenic, accusing.

"I said—only said—to warn her."

Though the trysts seemed obvious, neither Calogero, Domenic, nor his sons had actually caught Frances and Joe together.

"Warn," he repeated, as he walked past Domenic and into the church.

Domenic stared at the statue of the Virgin of Terrasini and prayed that Calogero would not call off the engagement. The loss of face would be too great, the loss of his sons' chances with the Romano gang too ill-timed.

But Calogero did not call off the engagement. And he did not speak of his suspicions with his fiancée. If the barber remained a problem, it would be a small one and he would deal with it. Calogero sat across the living room from his fiancée and looked ahead to the day when the priest would sanctify their marriage. Calogero was in love with Frances.

Chapter Eighteen ❧

Frances stood in Josie's wedding dress with tears streaming down her face, pleading with her mother as Concetta gathered a pinch of fabric at the waistline to gauge how much she'd have to take the dress in. The wedding day at the end of July was less than a month away.

"There is nothing to be done, Frances. It is settled. Get used to it."

"I'll never get used to it, Mama. I don't love him."

"Love will come later. And if not love, then respect."

"Do you love Papa, then?"

Concetta squinted at the fabric, and told Frances to turn.

"Most girls would give away their right thumb to be marrying Calogero Romano. Isn't he handsome enough? Tall enough? Rich enough?"

"Yes. Yes. Yes!" Frances' voice rose with each assent. "And he seems likeable enough, too, Mama. But he isn't Joe."

"Do not torture yourself your whole life for this, Francesca. Your insides will dry up and you'll make withered babies."

The following Saturday after dinner, Frances suddenly doubled over, grabbing at her stomach.

"Mama, help, I'm going to be sick."

Concetta shooed her off to the bathroom, telling Aggie and

Mary to get busy cleaning up the kitchen. When Frances finally emerged from the bathroom red-faced and shivering, Concetta put her cheek to Frances's forehead and then sent her straight to the dining room.

"Somebody must have given you the *malocchio*. Sit down and I'll take it away."

She dashed into the kitchen and returned with a shallow soup bowl filled with water in one hand, a tablespoon of olive oil in the other. Concetta snapped off a piece of palm from the looped fronds she'd tucked behind the crucifix on the dining room wall, and tossed it into the water before raising the bowl above Frances's head with her left hand.

She closed her eyes and began to mumble the secret prayer her mother had passed down to her at midnight one Christmas Eve when she was a girl, then opened her eyes. Three times she drew the sign of the cross on Frances's forehead with her right thumb.

"Get behind you the *malocchio*. God get in front of you to lead you through."

Then she swiped her thumb through the tablespoon of olive oil and watched as she let one drop fall into the water. It floated.

She swished her thumb in the water to rinse it. Again she recited the prayer and swiped the sign of the cross three times across Frances's forehead, and again she dripped one drop of oil into the water and watched it float. It was a good sign. A third time she repeated the ritual, but this time the drop of oil did not bead up. Instead, it merged with the other two drops of oil, spreading across the surface to make one large blob—an eye.

"Ach, the *malocchio*! I knew it. Someone is jealous of you."

She began again to intone the ancient cure below her breath, urging the evil eye to release her daughter from its spell. Then she made the sign of the cross over the water three times and swirled it with her fingers before tossing it down the kitchen sink.

Again she returned to the dining room, with a fresh bowl of water, and performed the entire ritual once more. This time all three drops fell and floated free. Perfect. Concetta made the sign of the cross across her own chest and set the bowl on the table for Frances to see before she tossed the mixture down the sink.

"Now, to bed with you. Everything will be fine in the morning, you'll see."

But in the morning, when her sisters rose to dress for Mass, Frances rolled onto her side, drew her knees to her chest, and moaned.

"It hurts too much, I can't get up," she whimpered as Concetta sat down on the bed to check Frances's face for fever.

"You're too sick for church? Maybe if you sit up and eat something it will pass. I'll bring you some—"

Frances cut her off. "No, Mama, I can't. If I eat something I'll only throw it up again. I feel so dizzy, just let me sleep."

"She's too sick to go to church," Concetta replied, answering the question in Domenic's raised eyebrows when everyone but Frances had gathered in the front hallway to leave for Mass. Concetta slipped her beige purse over her arm and picked at a piece of lint on Sal's pants, then gestured toward the door with both hands.

"*Andiamo*, let's get going before we are late. She'll be fine by herself for an hour. Poor thing already fell back to sleep."

Calogero stood waiting for them in the shade outside the church and frowned while Domenic waved off his concern over Frances's ailment.

"No, no. It's nothing. You know these women. You'll see. She'll be fine by the time you come for dinner."

The Costas slid into their pew, Domenic pulling out his hanky and wiping off the bench before he sat down. Calogero stepped in last, taking the aisle seat. He fidgeted in his seat for a few minutes, turning to glance behind them several times as the altar boy swept out in his black and white vestments and began to light the tall tapers. Finally, Calogero leaned toward Rocco and whispered, "You seen the Falcos this morning?"

Rocco turned to scan the congregants seated behind them. Finally he spotted old man Falco and his wife with their two daughters, but there was no sign of Joe Falco in the pew beside them.

"We're out of here," Rocco said, jumping to his feet so quickly he nearly shoved Calogero into the aisle.

Calogero slammed his limousine against the curb and he and Rocco charged up the stairs to the Costa girls' bedroom, their leather shoes making thunder on the wood. The bedroom door was ajar, and for a moment they halted in the doorway, taken aback. Frances was right there, in her bed, huddled beneath the summer-weight blanket.

Rocco moved toward the bed and leaned over to look at his sister, but her head was hidden under the covers. He lifted the thin blanket and he roared. Calogero was at the bed in two steps. His jaw began to clench.

Sheets and pillows pulled from their cases were wadded beneath the blanket where Frances should have been.

Rocco lunged for her *cassete* at the foot of the bed and flung open the lid. It sat nearly empty.

It was Calogero who spotted his engagement ring glittering on the top of the girls' dresser.

"Find her."

Rocco rubbed his eyes and tried to think while Calogero drove for his father's house. Calogero had vetoed running back to Holy Family Church to get Pasquale and Angelo and Domenic. No need for every goddamn dago from here to Gratiot and Harper to know his business, especially the priest who was set to marry them. He could take care of himself. He had plenty of other men to send looking.

"They can't have gotten that far," Rocco offered. "The question is, where are they headed? Or hiding?"

"Shut it, will you? Just goddamn think. Who does Falco have who would run them out of Detroit? Who are his guys?"

"I say we drive by the barbershop, and if they aren't there, we try the sonofabitch's house. We'll get to his father just about when he walks in from church."

Frances and Joe were not at the barbershop and they weren't at the Falco home, either. Beads of sweat soaked the old barber's shirt collar as he swore on the Virgin's eyes that he'd had no hint of the couple's *fuitina*.

"None. Nothing," his wife said, shivering in the July heat. "How could they elope? Look. The car is still in front of the house."

"But his goddamn clothes are missing," Rocco shouted from the top of the hall stairs.

"And so is my fiancée."

Calogero didn't have to tell the Falcos he would be watching their house and the barbershop. They already knew that from today, the Romano gang would know to the penny how much Falco made each day, what his family ate for dinner, and how many times they wiped their *culos*.

Josie prayed for her sister morning and night. Her father heard rumors that the Romanos had combed the neighborhoods along Dixie Highway from Detroit down into Toledo and questioned the operators of the ferryboat services running between Detroit and Windsor with similar results. That they also checked out the trains that roared to Canada through a tunnel the railroad bored beneath the Detroit River to carry cargo and sometimes passengers, to no avail. My grandmother's brother suspected they'd even requested cooperation from the cops they paid to look the other way when a shipment came across the river. No one was talking.

Domenic had little to say, either. He searched for Frances also, with his sons, and he roiled with anger. His daughter had besmirched his honor, blackened his family's face. Where could he go without encountering derision in the eyes of the *christiani?* His stature diminished, Domenic began to spend Sunday afternoons at home, unwilling to play bocce and have to face the knowing eyes of his *cumparis.*

And his reputation as a *consigliere?* Completely compromised. His daughter's betrayal had instantly devalued any counsel he could offer to powerful men who expected from him the advice of a Solomon. If his own daughter would not abide by his word, why would the capos expect anyone else to? In the two months since Frances and Falco disappeared, he had put on a suit and gone to church on Sundays and he had hitched his horse to the new wagon and gone to work the rest of the week. After he fed the horse he sat down to his own dinner, then headed back to the garage to brush and water the weary animal. Every morning when he mucked out the garage, he tossed the fresh manure onto the pile growing at the back fence where Falco had co-opted his daughter.

He was grateful for the continuing presence of Calogero Romano and troubled by it at the same time. Domenic was grateful that his sons hadn't been given the boot by Calogero's father, but every moment in Calogero's company was heavy with the disgrace Frances had brought upon her family. It was driving him crazy. *Why couldn't anyone find her?*

Lest anyone suppose he was relinquishing his claim on Frances Costa, Calogero sat tall in the aisle seat alongside her family every Sunday morning at Holy Family Church and he choked down the bread he broke at the Costas' dinner table every Sunday afternoon while he struggled to avert his gaze from Frances's empty chair. Calogero wanted nothing more than for Frances to come walking through her father's front door. He told her father that he could forgive Frances anything.

Calogero looked straight into Domenic's eyes and told him that he was in love with her.

Chapter Nineteen ❧

Aunt Grace leads me by the hands.

Detroit, 1993

My search for my grandmother's lost sister began in Aunt Grace's kitchen the morning she showed me the obliterated name in my great-grandfather's passport, and it consumed more than a decade. Even though I was torn by how distraught my grandmother was, I pressed Grace to divulge more. Grace told me the first of the many versions I'd come to hear about what happened to Frances.

"Who killed her?"

"Her brother!" she spits out, disdain screwing up her face, pale now, the color of her champagne hair. "Hey, no one told me, either," she says, more to her mother than to me. "Not until after we went camping out west and I made Uncle Sam take a detour so I could take my kids to visit Uncle Rocco."

I nod, knowing Grace would have caught hell had she not gone out of her way to show her uncle *rispetto*.

"When I came back, everyone sneered and asked why the hell I took time from my vacation to go see my 'favorite uncle.' "

My horror deepens. Grace's sarcastic inflection on "favorite uncle" indicts Rocco.

"Gramma's brother?"

"And the other one, too. Pasquale."

I have to sit down. My grandmother says nothing. She sits there looking as if she's about to have a stroke.

"Why?"

Grace sits at the table now, too.

"They made her marry an older man. But she didn't love him. She used to sneak into the alley to see the young barber she was in love with. Her brothers warned her not to, but she did it anyway. One day they caught her, and they got rid of her for dishonoring the family."

Now my head also starts to wag back and forth like my grandmother's as I struggle to process this information.

"How? How did they 'get rid' of her?"

"Belle Isle."

Grace names the lush island park in the Detroit River and I picture its Scott Fountain, that magical confection with its mist fine as a wedding veil, the backdrop for my mother's and Grace's and thousands of other brides' wedding portraits.

"They took her there and they threw her in and drowned her." She says it as if she's reporting the temperature outside, but I can't get my thoughts past those family wedding pictures and picnics and canoe rides at Belle Isle to factor in a murder.

Grace pauses, raising her eyebrows for effect. She has more.

"And you can imagine what they did to her first."

I force myself to block images of rape before they can coalesce. I close my mind to everything except the hideous realization that I have the blood of murderers flowing in my veins.

I scoop up the box of papers, with the promise to return as soon as I've copied them at the Speedy Printer store a half mile away. I know better than to ask if I can hang on to the documents.

That morning was the last time anyone opened the mildewed box. Some years later, it was pitched into the garbage along with the other mementos that perished in the flood in Aunt Grace's basement.

Chapter Twenty ❧

Detroit, 1919

Frances's and Calogero's July wedding day came and went without a trace of her or her barber. Concetta ran her fingers over the tiny faux pearls and flowers she had added to Josie's veil and wept quiet tears for her lost daughter. She prayed to the Virgin to keep her safe. She prayed to Saint Anthony, patron saint of lost things, to bring her home, even though she feared what might happen if she came.

Summer simmered into fall, and Frances's sixteenth birthday also passed without a word from her. Still Concetta did not give up hope of seeing her second daughter again. There was still the laundry to do, dinner to cook, a house to keep up, and sometimes, briefly, she found herself distracted from worry.

One afternoon when she had run out of yeast, Concetta sent her ten-year-old, Louie, running down the street to the corner store to pick some up. He plunked down his change, grabbed the little paper bag, and had turned to leave when he noticed a girl from his class in the small store. She was standing just inside the doorway with two men. She didn't react when Louie gave her a small smile of recognition as he passed her.

Two days later the school was in shock; teachers and students walked the hallways in stunned horror. Louie's little classmate had been found strangled. Her father, the story went, had been unable to come up with the increasing sum of money he owed to a gang that had long run out of patience. "Our money or your kid," the ransom note had said, but as he frantically scrabbled together a few dollars, he never believed they would murder a ten-year-old girl.

Louie couldn't concentrate on his schoolwork. He couldn't eat. He couldn't sleep. He couldn't get his classmate out of his mind. Or the two men he'd seen with her inside the front door of the neighborhood store.

Two men in crisp fedoras and three-piece suits showed up on the Costas' doorstep the following week, asking for Domenic and the young boy who had run his mama's errand. Louie stood close to his father on the front porch. The men looked into his eyes and smiled at him.

"You didn't happen to see a little girl in the store last week when you went shopping for your mama, did you?"

Louie looked confused.

"Little girl?" He shook his head. "I don't know anything about a little girl."

"You didn't see a little girl in the store?"

Louie lifted his shoulders in a quick shrug. "No. I don't remember any little girl."

"You didn't see two men in the front of the store? Two men with a little girl? Think now. Be sure."

Louie squinted, as if trying to search his memory, before he answered.

"No, I don't remember any men or any little girl."

One of the men, the lieutenant of the gang that had kidnapped Louie's little classmate, reached out and ruffled Louie's brown curls.

"Good boy," he said. He smiled at Domenic and extended his hand in congratulations. "Your son is going to grow up to be a fine Mafioso one day."

Chapter Twenty-one ❧

Detroit, 1993

Your father went to his *grave* and never knew that goddamned
shit!" My mother was roaring her outrage into the phone,
even before I could finish asking if everything Aunt Grace had
told me was true. "Forget about it, right now, you hear me? I cannot believe she told you that rotten bunch of shit."

I reeled, sucker punched.

Secrets, we all have them. The dark places within ourselves
we'd rather keep as undisturbed as a grave, the skeletons that
dance through the generations, rattling their bones from time to
time lest their descendants forget what others still living don't
want them to remember.

But to keep this from my father . . . ?

The extent to which this secret had been concealed rivaled the
horror of Frances's murder. There was nothing my mother could
have revealed to her Ray that would have made him adore her
less. *What would people think?* That old Sicilian worry. My father
was her closest friend, the love of her life, her anchor for more
than forty-two years. My father wasn't *people.*

My mother kept other secrets. All Italians do. Some are innocuous
bits of nonsense that eventually bubble up like the laughter they
produce.

The worthy ones, the secrets of consequence, swallow up the tongues of the living until they sleep together in the grave. Unseen forces, nevertheless they twist and mold unsuspecting lives, bruise and batter bewildered souls. *Omerta*—what happens in the "family" stays in the family. Powerful, percolating, persistent, these insidious secrets are the ones I fear.

"Karen Ann, did you hear me?" my mother asks, rage making her growl now. "Forget this. Drop it. Leave it alone. I don't want to hear another word about it, do you understand?"

I knew I was hearing her fear, more than her anger. Shame and stigma had long ago purchased her silence.

"But what did she do?" I asked. "Aunt Grace said she used to sneak into the alley to see the barber she was in love with after they made her marry an older man."

"No, she had hot pants, that one," my mother said, disgust in her voice. "She was engaged to the older one but kept meeting the young one in the alley. Her brothers warned her several times to cut it out."

"They killed her for talking to a boy in the alley?"

"She was warned, and that's all I'm going to say about it. That's it. I never want you to bring this rotten shit up again. It's been dead and buried all these years, and it should have stayed that way. Leave it alone."

I promised my mother nothing, imagining I could easier stop breathing than I could leave it alone.

Chapter Twenty-two ❖

Detroit, 1919

It was an evening in mid-October while her parents and Aggie and Sal were sitting on the front porch that Frances appeared suddenly, a tall straight figure slipping silently from the shadows of dusk to the approach of their front walk. She stood alone.

"Francesca!"

The word was a knife slicing into the night. Domenic rose to face her. With his shirtsleeves rolled above the elbows and hands splayed on his thighs, he was a silhouette of coiled, compact energy waiting to strike.

"*Si*, Papa. It is." Frances's voice was even, flat. She hung back, but she did not cower under his scrutiny. She wore a store-bought dress with a long bodice, short sleeves, and a straight skirt that skimmed her knees. Her head was held high, her gaze direct, her demeanor quietly defiant. A slim gold band circled her left ring finger.

"What is on your hand? *Veni ca.* Come. To me." It was an order, not a request.

It seemed Frances shifted her posture to stand straighter but she made no move toward him.

"*Dio*, please," Concetta whispered, squeezing her eyes shut in supplication. Aggie and Sal stood motionless beside her. Tension thick as dusk had stolen their breath.

"You heard your father, whore. Go!" Rocco ordered as he bolted through the front door.

"*Basta*," Domenic barked, raising an arm to silence his son. "Enough. I know how to handle my own family."

"I came to see you," Frances began, "to tell you that I am married."

"I see you," Domenic snorted, answering her English in kind. "I will see you in hell, that's where I'm going to see you. Disgrace to your family. Disgrace to your *fidanzato*. Disgrace to our honor."

With each sentence he advanced on her, but she stood her ground.

"Run, eh? Far enough you didn't run." His voice was loud enough for neighbors to hear. "You had no sense and I should have beat it into you. You! Handed more *fortuna* than any of us. But no! You are a stupid girl, Frances. A *puttana*. Calogero Romano—he wasn't good enough for my daughter, the whore?"

He cuffed Frances across the face so hard that Concetta heard her daughter's neck snap. Frances tottered backward and regained her footing, staring her father down.

She gulped for air, sobs choking her words.

"You would have married me to an old man I didn't love. Not for me. For you. You wanted it only for your sons!" she cried, raising her chin toward Rocco.

The muscles along Rocco's jaws tensed, but Frances knew he wouldn't dare move from the porch into his father's domain.

"Filthy whore!" Domenic screamed. "Fish-smelling cunt! I could kill you. I will teach you what it means to respect your family." His next blow knocked her to the ground.

"No!" Sal screamed. "Papa, stop! Get up, Frances, run. Run away."

"Get into the house," Domenic ordered, yanking her to her feet. "You've done enough running." At that moment he tightened his grip and met the resistance of rounded metal, the golden wedding band on Frances's finger. "I could kill you," he screamed, over and over, pushing Frances up the stairs.

Aggie and Sal sidled against Concetta whimpering, but Rocco merely smirked. Satisfaction glinted in his dark eyes as his sister stumbled up the stairs. There was something shiny all over Frances's face, running down her cheeks in a trail too wide and dark to be tears.

Inside, Concetta rinsed a washcloth in cold water and handed it to Frances for her face before Domenic ordered her from the room.

"All of you, out."

From the other side of the kitchen door, Concetta and her children listened as Domenic slammed his hand on the table and grilled Frances. She and her husband had returned to his parents' home this afternoon, but she'd insisted on coming to her home alone. It was time to come back and make peace with their families, they'd decided, but she'd told Joe that she was the one who had to speak with her father first.

Domenic did not lay another hand on her, but in the hour that they talked, the anger never left his voice. When there was nothing left to say, Frances rose from her chair and told him she needed to get back to her husband.

Pasquale had come down into the dining room, and Mary and Louie and Mike were crowded around the table with their mother, too, waiting to see Frances.

"Even a *puttana* doesn't walk back to her husband's family's house alone in the dark," Rocco said as the kitchen door opened. "Pasquale and I will drive you back there."

Chapter Twenty-three ❧

Detroit, 1993

I couldn't let it go. I couldn't *not* ask. None of it made sense to me. What were Gramma and Mama protecting? They didn't kill Frances. And the brothers who had were long dead.

The one thing I did know—remembering how my grandmother's face had flushed with anguish, how her blood pressure had risen to turn her ears bright red—was that I couldn't ever ask *her*.

I went back to my mother. Each time I ventured a question about Frances with her, Mama's face soured with scowls identical to those she favored me with on Sunday mornings when I skipped back downstairs from tea and toast and tattling to her widowed nemesis.

My Grandma Tintori taught me to be a good reporter when I was barely four or five. While I watched her pack loose tea in the metal strainer, hang it over the pot's lip to steep, and then slant bread against the coils of her toaster and latch them inside the metal doors, she asked me to answer four of the "five Ws" (and an H)—who, what, where, when, and how. Grandma Tintori relied on herself to supply the "why."

Inevitably, my parents would chastise me for letting my namesake "pump me," for spilling my guts about innocuous things I had no idea weren't mine to share—who'd come for dinner or telephoned, where we had gone. But they never forbade me to go upstairs to visit.

I wonder now if they glanced nervously up at the ceiling, at each other, each time I tromped out the kitchen door and up the back staircase, worrying about what I'd exchange this weekend for tea and toast and stories about the Illinois coal towns where my American-born grandmother had lost her youth.

During the decade when I sought the truth about Frances, my mother not only grew accustomed to my search, she offered tidbits of her youth and asked if I was going to write about them. She told me once she had secrets of her own, that she would tell me about them over lunch one day.

I immediately made a date with her for the following week.

We lingered over coffee and dessert and the subject never surfaced. Finally, I got up the nerve to ask her.

"Secrets? What secrets? I never told you I had any secrets."

Chapter Twenty-four ⚜

Detroit, 1919

Concetta was on the davenport in the front room sewing in dim
light when Rocco and Pasquale returned home.

"Ah, there you are." Her needle paused in midflight. "Already
I was getting worried. . . ."

"You saw Falco?" Domenic called down from the top of the
hall stairs.

"It is taken care of," Rocco said. "There is honor in this house.
From today, honor."

Concetta noticed the bloody shirt balled up in Rocco's hand
and realized for the first time that he was bare-chested. She began
to scream, a low, wounded moan that circled the room, trailing
Rocco and Pasquale as they began to empty one picture frame after another, hurling them aside in a crescendo of breaking glass.
The moan gave way to inhuman howls ululating above the thunder of her eldest sons' hurried footsteps on the staircase, of drawers
crashing open and doors slamming closed.

"Mama? Papa?" Other voices, tentative, young, called through
the house. "What is the matter, Mama?"

Awakened from a sound sleep, Aggie and Mary sat upright in
their nightgowns and trembled. At the first crash of glass, ten-
year-old Louie had scooted under the bed with Sal and Mikey.
Hidden there, the youngest boys watched their mother stagger to
their parents' room across the darkened hallway and collapse

against her dresser. Howling, she yanked open the bottom drawer and fell to her knees, clutching the wedding dress to her bosom, rocking and wailing a raw and bottomless pain. She ignored her husband and Rocco and Pasquale as they pillaged the bedrooms, snatching pictures and papers, turning closets and dressers on end. She only bellowed out that savage howl, ripping the lace to shreds like a lioness tearing at a fresh kill. Clawing, she flung herself around their papa's ankles when he and their older brothers finally tore the gown away from her.

Louie shoved his fist into his mouth to gag his whimpers as he watched his father struggle toward the stairs with Concetta hanging on his ankles with a death grip. Goggle-eyed, he watched his father try to kick her off, then drag her with him across the hallway floor. He kept on down the stairs, thumping her face-first behind him, finally kicking himself free of her when he'd hobbled halfway down to the foyer. Louie cowered beneath his bed long after his father and brothers stormed to the basement with Frances's wedding dress. His clothes were cold with urine when he finally slid out, shaking so badly he could barely creep down to the basement stairs.

The coal furnace blazed with an orange and greedy mouth, consuming everything they'd found of hers. Louie watched Rocco fling his mother to the floor as she tried to tear a picture from the pile of Frances's things that her sons and husband were feeding to the furnace. He covered his ears to block his mother's screams and ran back upstairs to the bedroom where Sal and Mikey were still curled beneath the bed.

Angelo came home in the midst of the purging and joined his father and brothers at the furnace, making shorter the work of wiping out any trace of Frances.

Remembering the shoe box filled with birth certificates and other documents that his father kept in the bedroom closet, Angelo dashed upstairs to retrieve it.

"The *documenti*," he announced, as he began rifling through them for Frances's birth and baptismal papers. They curled to ash moments after Domenic threw them into the furnace.

"The passport!" Domenic's face registered alarm. He grabbed up the small booklet. It was issued in his name, but Concetta and every one of their children from Angelo down was listed in it by name, age, and birthplace. Only Rocco and Pasquale, whom he'd left in Detroit in 1914, were missing.

Angelo opened the book and scanned the list to find Frances's name. Then, licking the lead of the pencil he carried in his back pocket, he scribbled her out of the family.

Chapter Twenty-five ✤

Concetta endured her days like a robot, plagued by excruciating headaches. Her children came home from school to find her wandering the neighborhood, tearing at her hair as if it were the cause of her suffering. She sliced potatoes and tied them to her forehead with a strip of cloth, believing the vegetable would root out her pain.

No one spoke of Frances. Not Concetta's family, not her *cummaris*, not her friends. It was as if her beautiful daughter had never existed.

There was no communication with the Falco family, not even eye contact in church. No one commented on the whereabouts of Joe Falco, either.

Louie thought about Frances every day. She was his favorite sister, the one Rocco had kicked, the one who would buy him an ice cream if she had a nickel. He liked to think about Frances. It made him want to kill Rocco and Pasquale for what they'd done to her.

He couldn't get the sight of that little kidnapped girl out of his mind, either. He fantasized that he could have saved her from those two men that afternoon, somehow. He pictured her strangled, and he heard in his head, over and over, the words the Mafioso had said to his father.

"Your son will grow up to be a fine Mafioso one day."

.   .   .

Concetta became preoccupied with Aggie, who had taken a fancy to a man Pasquale had brought home from the auto plant. Like Calogero, he was older. Like Calogero, he'd been calling every Sunday. Aggie was almost fifteen, but though Domenic had agreed to a courtship, he had some reservations about Paul Licata. He was a hard worker, he still lived at home with his parents, and he was connected with a powerful Mafia gang. But Domenic suspected that, while he showered Agata with attention on Sundays, the thirty-year-old laborer was sharing his affections elsewhere during the week. For now, he was going to keep his eye on Paul Licata.

While Licata proved himself, Domenic was already at work on a match for Mary. He'd taken a liking to Gino Giglia, with whom he'd made acquaintance at the bocce court. He, too, was much older than thirteen-year-old Mary, but Domenic knew Giglia had no family in Detroit, only a steady job and bocce ball to occupy his time. Mary thought Gino was an extremely handsome, gregarious man. When his clear blue eyes crinkled as he smiled at her, she was lost. She didn't dare raise her hopes, however, for there was no way her papa would consider entertaining a suitor for her until Aggie was officially engaged. When Domenic announced that both his daughters should dress themselves up for male callers one Sunday, Mary could hardly button her shoes, her fingers were trembling so over her good fortune.

As fall approached, Aggie grew restless for a *conuscenza* party, but her father's blessing was not forthcoming. Paul Licata pressured her to leave with him. With his connections, he told her, no one would dare blink an eye at them when they returned.

A week before Thanksgiving, she slipped down the back stairs in the middle of the night with hardly more than the clothes on her back, and like her sister Frances, she eloped.

The Costa household awoke to hysteria, as Domenic bellowed

and his sons raced out the door with him to track the couple down. Three days later, they found Aggie and Paul, properly married by the church and living with Paul's parents.

Concetta rolled out some sweet *sfinci* dough and drizzled the little fried balls with cinnamon and honey, Domenic bagged up one of his better bottles of red wine, and together the Costas went to their new *cumparis'* home to recognize their daughter's *fuitina* and marriage. There was no other choice. What was done was done, and at least Agata hadn't left them with the dishonor of a spurned *fidanzato*, as Frances had.

That night, Mary settled into bed alone for the first time in her life. Concetta tucked her in with a heavy heart, knowing the kind of life her Aggie would have with Licata—the same one she'd had with Domenic. Had leaving Corleone for America really brought a better life for her daughters?

Chapter Twenty-six ❧

Detroit, mid-1990s

On days I felt gutsy enough to provoke my mother's ire, I pressed her for more details about Frances's disappearance. She told me once that her uncles had caught Frances with boys in the alley and had beaten her, warning her to stop.

I called her on that. If my great-grandfather had beaten my grandmother so severely for handing her fiancé his hat, Frances's brothers wouldn't have let her off with only a beating and a warning if they'd caught her in a sexually compromising situation in the alley.

"Oh, yes," my mother told me. "They warned her more than once."

I wasn't buying it.

Chapter Twenty-seven ❧

My grandparents with their firstborn, my mother.

Detroit, 1921

For Concetta, one day of distress blended with the next. Daily, she mourned her second daughter, feared her grown sons and worried about them, and gave her headaches over to raw potatoes. Not even the news that finally, after five years of marriage, Josie was expecting Nino's first child, seemed to faze Concetta. Besides, the baby would be named after Nino's side.

Late in the summer of 1921, my mother, Giovannina Mazzarino, entered the world as the Costa family's second American citizen and its first baby born in a hospital. Named after Nino's mother, she was also the first female in her family ever born with the right to vote when she turned eighteen. She was a round-faced infant with a small rosebud mouth, almond-shaped brown eyes, and a head covered with dark peach fuzz. The minute Josie pulled back her crocheted blanket to introduce her to uncles Louie, Sal, and Mikey, Giovannina became their pet project. At eleven, ten, and six, Josie's youngest brothers fell easily into the role of Giovannina's big brothers—and in no time, her tormentors.

Before she began to crawl, Giovannina's uncle Rocco had taken himself a wife, and her grandmother Concetta's worst fears had come to pass—Giovannina's uncle Angelo had become the first Costa arrested by the Detroit police. Apprehended in an auto neither he nor his accomplice, Rafaele, owned, Angelo was cuffed, shoved into the police wagon, and pushed into the station, where the cops booked him for auto theft. Domenic went to Nino for the two thousand dollars he needed to bail Angelo out, Rafaele's family came up with his two thousand, and a German bondsman promised the court the two would appear for trial.

Baby Giovannina's peach fuzz refused to grow beyond a few long wisps of hair. Numerous afternoons as they cut fresh pasta or hung out the wash, Josie and Concetta and the *cummaris* fretted over it. Concetta had even pierced her granddaughter's ears with a needle and string when she turned six months, so that the *christiani* would realize she was a girl. Overhearing one of the *cummaris* tell his mother that if you shave hair it will grow back thick and fast, Louie ran to the bathroom for Domenic's shaving mug and brush. He carefully lifted his father's straight razor from its shelf in the medicine cabinet and sharpened the blade by running it up and down the thick leather strap that hung beneath the mug, same as he'd seen his father do. Equipment in hand, Louie harped at Sal and Mikey to stop Giovannina from wriggling while he lathered up her little head and shaved it bald.

Angelo's and Rafaele's trial was perfunctory and quick, netting them each a sentence of four to ten in Jackson State Prison for unlawfully driving away an auto. Angelo had just turned twenty-three. His prison intake records indicate that he was medium tall, with heavy eyebrows, deep narrow eyes, full thick lips, and gonorrhea. It noted that the middle finger of his left hand had been amputated to his palm—which my mother years later insisted was from an assembly line accident and not a Mafia "punishment." That she volunteered this information so adamantly made it suspect.

My mother told me that her earliest childhood memories went back to that time, when she was less than two years old. She vividly remembered the three-hour car rides upstate to Jackson prison, and sitting on her mother's lap beside her grandparents to visit with her favorite uncle.

Once Josie became pregnant with Giovannina, her other children followed in quick succession. By the end of the year, Giovannina had a baby brother, Dom, named for Josie's father because Nino refused to have any son of his bear his father's name.

Giovannina's hair grew back, but sparse as ever. Next, her young uncles decided to pull a floral cap down on her head so she wouldn't be mistaken for a boy. By the time she was three her hair had grown in straight, dark, and fine. Her mother cut it ear length, with bangs, and with her dark, almond-shaped eyes, Giovannina resembled an Asian waif.

Three months after her third birthday, the family's visits to Jackson prison ended. After serving two and a half years of his sentence, Angelo had won parole. Domenic told Concetta to cook a huge family dinner to welcome Angelo home, but ten minutes after he inhaled his first home-cooked pasta in thirty months he was back out on the streets with his brothers and buddies.

.　　.　　.

While Louie and his younger brothers got up before dawn to serve Mass, their older brothers spent all their free time whoring, drinking, and rumrunning. Sometimes the Costa boys drove the gang cars across the frozen river. Other times they stole vehicles they could abandon if they suspected they were being tailed. Many nights they'd roll in from a speakeasy or a trip across the river only long enough to collapse for a few hours' sleep before they needed to be alert and present on the assembly line.

Concetta and Domenic were proud that their three youngest were altar boys at Holy Family Church, but did not understand Louie's obsession with being allowed to read the Bible on his own, to study it without an intercessor. He carried out his duties as an altar boy, filling the chalices, one with water, one with wine, and he lit the altar candles and brought the priests their freshly laundered sacramental garb, but·he was frustrated. He had friends at school who attended the Protestant Italian church, who went to Bible study classes, who didn't listen to the pope.

Sometimes as he helped the priests don their vestments before Mass, he would ask them a question about the Bible, but the priests shushed him with a dismissive wave, telling him to concentrate on his prayer book. They were the ones ordained to deliver the words of the Gospels and Epistles to the congregation from the pulpit. He was to listen. Reading the Bible was reserved for them.

Louie's growing disenchantment with the church turned to disillusionment on Easter Sunday when he arrived to dress for Mass to find the priests in a drunken stupor. Try as he might to garb them in their vestments, to prop them up and get them to the altar, he barely succeeded. He hung up his altar boy cassock for the last time after that Easter Sunday Mass, and went home to tell his parents he'd become a Protestant.

Concetta crossed herself and exclaimed to God and the Virgin in horror. Domenic forbade him to go to the other church. But Louie was a teenager, and he was having none of it. His days as a

Catholic were over. At the Protestant church, he said, he was free to question, free to learn. He was going to a church where he was free to read the Bible, and no one was stopping him.

Within several months, his younger brothers had hung up their own altar boy cassocks to join him. They hungrily turned toward Jesus and away from the life their older brothers led.

Chapter Twenty-eight ❖

My mom, Jenny, in her final school photo, in ninth grade.

Nino had watched his father-in-law's ice cream and popcorn business with growing interest, and now, with two children and a pregnant wife to support, he decided he would work for himself, too. He had a green thumb and loved toiling in his garden, but didn't have land enough to grow profitable quantities of produce to sell. He loved the Sicilian-run Eastern Market, too, which always reminded him of home. He knew quality produce, and if he couldn't grow it, he could still sell it. He told Josie he was going to follow her father's lead. They couldn't afford a horse yet, so Nino bought a pushcart and walked it through the neighborhoods until he'd squirreled away enough for a horse. The children squealed with surprise when their papa rode home two months later with a brown horse he named Tom.

Every morning, Nino rose before the stars slipped from the sky to feed Tom and hitch him to the cart so they'd arrive at Eastern Market when the pickings were the choicest, just after the three hundred farmers who rented its stalls had pulled up their buggies and set out their bushels, between 3 and 4 A.M. Nino then spent an hour or more wandering from farmer to farmer, and to the other hundred vendors, making mental notes as he surveyed the day's crops. Once he'd settled on whose bushels he wanted on his cart, the haggling would begin. Often he and a buddy would go in on a bushel of beans or cucumbers and then play a game of *morra* to see which of them would divide it in half.

By daybreak, with his purchases paid for and loaded on, Nino would climb into the driver's seat and direct Tom to their route— the Jewish neighborhoods east of Woodward Avenue and south of Grand Boulevard. House to house he hawked his produce along the tree-lined boulevards, selling a peck of tomatoes here, weighing up a pound of beans there, choosing the ripest melons somewhere else. Some days he would sell out of almost everything, bringing back to Josie for their next day's dinner only those fruits and vegetables that wouldn't keep on the cart for tomorrow.

Usually, it was the ripest cantaloupes. He'd carry them into the kitchen, fragrant with sweet perfume, and while Josie lifted her sleepy children from their beds to see their papa, he'd slice the melons open, scoop out the seeds, and fill their orange craters with mounds of ice cream for an evening snack. Chocolate ice cream was the best, Giovannina decided, sitting in her nightgown at the kitchen table. Savoring the interplay of warm and cold, tangy and sweet, firm and melty, parent and child, she loved listening to her papa tell them of his day's adventures. When their little tummies bulged full, Nino would kiss his children's sticky faces goodnight before Josie returned them to their beds and then turned down Nino's and hers. For a woman who'd married with no clue about sex, she had caught on with gusto in a hurry. Many nights, even late into her pregnancies, she would try to rouse Nino from his sleep for a second go, and come daytime, she was never shy about tossing out sexual innuendos or bantering about lovemaking with her female friends.

Nino came home from peddling one night to find his mother-in-law humming in his kitchen while she cooked him pasta. Josie was in the hospital with their new baby, a healthy son they would baptize Saverio.

Her next pregnancy ended in tragedy. Two days before she went into labor, Josie became frightened when the baby who had been so active for so long suddenly stopped moving. He was born beautiful and blue, with the umbilical cord wrapped twice around his tiny neck. Josie was confined to the hospital, so, alone, Nino accompanied the tiny casket to Mount Olivet Cemetery and watched as the grave digger buried his third son, James, in the row of tiny unmarked graves along the fence.

The fall after Giovannina started school, Josie popped out another daughter, Constance, named to honor Concetta. Although Giovannina loved to play with her younger cousin Anna, Uncle Rocco's daughter, at family get-togethers, she was thrilled to finally claim a baby sister all her own.

By then, both of her aunts and her two eldest uncles were married, and she had numerous other cousins to play with at her grandparents' house. Giovannina loved school and quickly learned to speak English without any accent. At home she was Giovannina, an obedient child who answered her parents in Sicilian. At school, she was a voracious reader who spoke perfect English and told her classmates that her name was Jenny.

Jenny loved sharp pencils and the fresh sheets of paper she used to write out her homework. There was other homework she was responsible for, too, from a young age. Josie, like her mother, Concetta, was a firm believer that when God gave you daughters, He gave you extra pairs of hands—and the eldest daughter's hands held the biggest burdens. With cooking and laundry and so many small ones to take care of, Josie taught Jenny early on how to clean the house. Many days, after her eldest had made their own home spotless, Josie sent Jenny over to one of her *cummaris'* homes to do the same there.

Her uncle Angelo's freedom didn't last as long as the time he'd spent imprisoned. Jenny came home from school one March afternoon to find her mother crying while she floured chicken pieces for frying. There had been a fight, a bad one, and Angelo had been arrested for assault and battery. He'd violated his parole. He was going back to prison.

Two years later, Jenny cried along with her grandmother and mother and aunts. Her beloved uncle Angelo was getting out of prison again, but there was no celebration of his parole this time, no homecoming party. The State of Michigan had discharged him from prison with an order for deportation back to Sicily.

The family gathered on Monroe Street after their good-byes to Angelo, and Jenny joined in the wailing when her grandmother collapsed in sobs across her dining room table. Over and over, Concetta babbled that her baby was only twenty-nine and she would never see him again. None of them would. Jenny couldn't know that her grandmother was sobbing also for the daughter she would never see again—and that her *nonna* wept for two other daughters as well.

For her childless Aggie, who stood long into the night peering out her bedroom window, waiting until she spotted her husband returning from his whores before she would jump into their bed and feign sleep. Concetta wept, picturing the brute as he beat her daughter, bellowing that her cold feet proved that she'd been out of bed and at the window again. Jenny didn't know her grandmother was weeping also for her daughter Mary, whose handsome husband told her constantly that she was worthless and then pushed her, pregnant, down the basement stairs.

Jenny had seen the way her uncles disrespected their wives. How Auntie Aggie had turned into such a sour person, how Auntie Mary sat with such sad eyes. She never saw that kind of fear or sadness in her mother's eyes, because her father was a prince. He never raised a hand to her mother. He hardly raised his voice—even to his children. He didn't have to. She and her siblings knew better than to disobey or disrespect their parents. The only time Jenny heard him yell was when he shouted out numbers and flung out a corresponding amount of fingers while he stood in a circle with other men playing a game of *morra*. Her papa used his voice to whistle, to hum, and to sing.

Detroit, 1934

After a gap of a nearly a decade, Josie was pregnant for the sixth and final time. She delivered a healthy girl they named Grace, and then took to her bed for an entire year with double pneumonia. Josie was a firm believer in giving in to sickness. Often she had she told her children, "If you are sick and don't act like it, no one will believe you."

As the eldest at thirteen, Jenny hurried about the house the week that Grace was born, fixing dinner, cleaning up her siblings, and getting them off to bed and off to school. Within a week, Josie called Jenny to her sickbed and told her she was finished with school. She had learned enough; now she had to help out her family. She had to take over Mama's job, running the household, cooking, cleaning—whatever was necessary to care for her parents, her other siblings, and the newborn Grace.

That night, Jenny sobbed herself to sleep, crying about the injustice. School was her life. The work alone was oppressive for any young girl to take on, but the work she could manage. What she could not bear was being robbed of her school. She loved school. She loved learning. Her penmanship was perfect. She excelled at her classes. She had friends at school, friends who were not Sicilian. She had dreams.

Someone would come for her. She was in America. Children here belonged in school. But day after day, tears staining her cheeks, Jenny would find herself at the front room peering out and wondering. Why hadn't the truant officer come to the door to tell her parents they were wrong? Didn't anyone at school miss her? Please God, why doesn't the truant officer walk up those stairs and take me back to school?

Instead, she worked like Cinderella. Even after Josie got up from her bed in 1936 and took over a portion of the household responsibilities once more, Jenny did not return to school. Instead she spent her days learning to bake and cleaning first her family's house and then the houses of her mother's closest *cummaris*. Aunt Connie told me recently how sorry she always felt for her older sister and how hard my grandmother worked her. Josie never asked Jenny, she simply told her to go to this one's house to iron, to that one's house to bleach the wash and hang it out to dry. Jenny received no pay and little thanks, but Josie basked in the glory of her daughter's labor.

Late one afternoon when Jenny arrived to help her mother's friend Louisa with her household chores, she found the four children crying and by themselves and ran back to get her mother.

"We don't know where Mama is," the children insisted, when Josie arrived. "She wasn't here when we came home from school."

Josie sent Jenny back home to start their own dinner while she remained with her friend's children until their father came home.

His face contorted with anger when Josie told him that Jenny had found the children alone. In a rage, he searched the house from top to bottom, slamming doors and further frightening his children.

"She's done it then," he growled. "She said she would leave me and she did it!"

"No! It is impossible," Josie cried, stepping back from him, the hairs on her neck rising with the certainty that he was lying, that he'd killed his wife. "Louisa was my closest friend. She would never go away—no matter what—without saying good-bye to me."

In the week that followed Louisa's "abandonment" of her family, Carlo accepted the neighbor women's help with his children while he proudly showed their husbands the fine cement job he had done on the addition he'd just completed in his basement. And three months after Louisa "disappeared," Carlo brought home a pretty young wife of fifteen to care for him and his four children.

About the same time, just a mile away, a godmother was ascending a wooden porch for an arranged meeting with the mother of a young woman her godson had designs on marrying. From several preliminary bits of conversation to feel this woman out, she knew her chances were slim. As she entered the home and the mother locked the screen door behind her, the godmother reached back and unlocked the door. While the two women retreated to the kitchen for coffee and small chitchat before getting down to the delicate negotiation, two men—one brandishing a gun—ran up the front stairs and knocked.

As the godmother, godson, and his friend had hoped, the sixteen-year-old Sicilian girl in question went to see who was at the door. Before she could peer out, the godson burst through the door and shoved a handful of salt into her mouth as a gag to prevent her from screaming. He gathered her up, carried her to the waiting car, and whisked her to a home north of Detroit, in the neighborhood the Sicilians dubbed Cagalupo—the place so far away it's where the wolf goes to defecate.

He locked her in and held her there, maintaining a proper distance at the opposite side of the room. Day and night he professed his love, asking for her hand in marriage while telling her that no one else would have her because they would never believe he had not ruined her. It took ten days for her to agree.

Chapter Twenty-nine ❧

Detroit, 1930s and 1940s

Josie and Nino kept a close watch on their three girls' chastity, making sure they were chaperoned, most often by their unwilling brothers. People would talk, and no one wanted people talking about their family. Like her mother and grandmother and great-grandmother before her, Josie taught her girls to cook and bake and keep house, skills they would need when they had husbands and houses of their own. Though Nino worked through the Depression, things were tight, and Josie taught her girls to prepare pasta dozens of ways. There was pasta with fried cauliflower, pasta with fried broccoli, pasta with asparagus, pasta with onion and garlic, pasta with peas. She taught them to prepare eggs for dinner in the same way, frying up some onion and garlic in olive oil and sautéing a single vegetable until it was tender, then cracking eggs into the pan and scrambling it all together for a meal.

Like most immigrant Italians, Nino and Josie fared better than many during the Depression because they had not allowed themselves to get into debt. Italians eschewed credit—they'd had enough of that burden in Sicily. Only their houses were purchased on credit, and when mortgage payments were hard to meet, the *cumparis* helped one another.

Sundays were still spent with the extended family, and Jenny and her siblings had plenty of cousins to laugh and fight with after dinner. When they were especially lucky, the cousins saw each other during the week.

One afternoon, Josie and Mary had errands to run and decided it would be safe to leave their nine children at Concetta and Domenic's house with their uncle Rocco. Though he was still the cruelest of their brothers, he was the only adult available to help them out.

For hours that afternoon, the kids entertained themselves by propping an extension leaf from the dining room table against the sofa, using it to slide to the floor. All of a sudden the laughter turned to screams when Tommy climbed onto the board, it slid from its perch on the sofa, and he and the board came crashing down on little Margaret's hand, smashing her fingers.

The seven-year-old erupted in howls, bringing Uncle Rocco running in to put an end to the game.

"Let me see that," he demanded, grabbing Margaret's hand. He looked at her fingers and then dropped her arm, heading for the kitchen. "I know exactly what will fix you."

He took a pan from the cupboard, filled it with water, put it on the stove, turned on the gas, and waited for the bubbles to pop to the surface. Then he dragged Margaret into the kitchen, stuck her red, swollen fingers into the boiling water, and held them there while she screeched in pain and pleaded for him to let her go.

"There, now." He shoved her from the kitchen with a scowl. "That made it all better, didn't it?"

Although his sisters were horrified, they were afraid to complain.

Josie and Mary's kids were close, when Mary's husband allowed the families to visit each other. Nino was especially fond of his nephew Tommy, and on the weekends when his own boys were not interested, he would often invite him along to ride the route. Tommy marveled that the horse that shared his name was so smart, that he knew the route and the way back home, and that his uncle Nino really did fall asleep as Tom took him home. The days that Tommy or one of his own sons worked alongside him, Nino would send them running up the long sidewalks to take the housewives' orders and back again with the baskets of produce to collect their money. Sometimes, on Friday nights or Saturday afternoons, the Jewish housewives or their husbands would ask Nino or the boys to come inside and turn on a light, or light the stove, a task that their Shabbat—their day of rest—prevented them from doing.

But what Tommy liked best was watching his uncle at work at Eastern Market, zeroing in on the choicest of everything and then haggling with the farmers until it was his to resell. Only once in his life did he ever see his mild-mannered uncle Nino lose his temper—over a bushel of green beans that Nino had paid for and that another peddler absconded with and then denied taking. Tommy came home and told everyone how Uncle Nino had yanked it off the vendor's cart. The vendor yanked it back. And then Uncle Nino had hauled off and punched the other guy and took back his beans.

Jenny never went to Eastern Market with her father, but she was in the hallway off the kitchen one afternoon when she heard her father's voice at the side door, opposite and a few steps down from the doorway where she stood. The side door landing was the junction between the few stairs leading up to the kitchen hallway and the long staircase perpendicular to them that continued down into the basement.

Her father had come home loaded down with crates filled with watermelons and eggplants that he'd bought to sell the following week. Josie came to the hallway door also and bristled when she saw that Nino had brought home a helper, a black man who was heading down the basement stairs ahead of her husband.

"This is the best one you could find to help you with this?" she hollered down to Nino in Sicilian. "A *niggudi?*"

The black man deposited the heavy crate in the basement corner Nino indicated and then headed up the stairs for another load. He stopped at the landing, and with one hand on the screen door, turned a puzzled face to Josie up at the hallway door.

"Why?" he asked her in perfectly accented Sicilian, watching the color drain from her cheeks. "Is there something you find the matter with me?"

I chuckled the first time I heard this story from my mother, imagining my grandmother's shock when she was called out like this. I still smirk about it.

As a young child, I bristled at her racism. Every spring, my mother washed all the walls in our house, just as my grandmother did—probably a throwback to the spring whitewashing of the house in Sicily. Once or twice a year, they'd tear the house apart, pulling furniture from the walls and scrubbing baseboards and cleaning closets. For the heavy cleaning, they hired the help of a black woman we kids adored, Lucinda. My father would pick her up and take her home, and used to joke that people in other cars must have thought she had a white husband, because they both were about the same size, roly-poly.

Although the three women worked side by side, sharing the work equally, and we all sat down to lunch at the same table, even at five years old I cringed whenever my grandmother took Lucinda's dishes and utensils to the sink and scrubbed them out with cleanser, washing ours with only dish soap. Those were the only times I can remember being ashamed of my grandmother.

My grandfather did not share her sentiments. He was comfortable with the black men who worked at Eastern Market, just as he was comfortable going into the homes of Jews on Friday nights to turn on their lights when they were forbidden to, bragging to me when I was an adult that he had been their "Shabbos goy."

Chapter Thirty ❧

Detroit, mid-1990s

I went back to Aunt Grace for further details, and she repeated the story the second time pretty much like the first. A few months later, I went back to my mother, cautiously, curiously, and little by little she opened up.

"You're not going to write about this, are you?"

"I don't know if I'm going to write about it. I just want to know what happened."

She told me again that Frances was oversexed, that she couldn't resist "meeting boys in the alley" although she knew her brothers would beat her if she got caught.

"But you said she got caught, and they warned her," I protested. "They wouldn't have warned Frances. And warned her *again*. They'd have just killed her. How did they explain her disappearance?"

"They just said she had to go away. Everyone understood what that meant."

The next time she told me Frances's story, my mother said that she had unwillingly married the Mafioso who was twenty years older than she, but that she still pined for her young barber and sneaked into the alley to meet him. That her Mafioso husband went to his father-in-law and brothers-in-law and told them to make her stop.

"Why?" I asked. "Why would she listen to her father and

brother any more than to her husband?" The story didn't make sense.

Another time, as my mother told the story, Frances wasn't yet married to the Mafioso husband, but was still his fiancée, and he went to his future in-laws to ask them to warn her not to meet boys in the alley.

The story never came out the same way twice.

Chapter Thirty-one ❧

Detroit, 1941

Jenny's second chance at school didn't come until she was twenty, after her sister Connie had already graduated from high school and was working downtown. Their brothers had pounded a Kodak sign into the front lawn and started a business developing photographs in the basement, and their father had made enough money to graduate to a produce truck.

Nino still could not read—nor could he write—but he knew his way around Detroit and its suburbs from memorizing the landmarks. He carried in his wallet his alien registration card, his membership card in the Detroit Fruit Vendors Association, and a bona fide Michigan driver's license bearing his photograph and signed Antonino Mazzarino in an Italian script that belonged to someone else.

With just her eighth-grade education, Jenny was admitted to a business school downtown. She studied shorthand, typing, and accounting and graduated near the top of her class, but evenings and weekends she was still a house slave to her mother and her mother's friends.

On the weekends and evenings, everyone helped Dom and Sam with their photo business. They'd built their darkroom in the basement, but the work overflowed to the main floor. Each evening after dinner, the dining room table was overrun with envelopes that needed to be filled with their matching negatives and finished prints.

Gracie, the baby, was still in grade school.

It was the early forties, and women were wearing pants. Jenny was petite. An inch taller than her mother, she stood just five feet tall. She wore pants well, and had inherited from her grandmother Concetta an eye for fine tailoring and classic styles. She was expected to bring home the paycheck from her secretarial job and hand it over to her mother, and Josie gave her back a small amount of money to buy clothes.

Though she and Connie rode the bus downtown unescorted, dating was an entirely different matter. The Sicilian community had tongues—and no one was going to talk about the Mazzarinos' daughters. If Jenny accepted a date, her brothers rode along as backseat chaperones.

There was an engagement—broken—and a string of suitors before Jenny decided to tell her parents enough was enough. She was sick of dating under her brothers' watchful eyes. The chance came just as her uncle Sal was getting married. Jenny returned from work to find her mother on the phone with her grandmother, and both of them in a lather.

Josie thudded the black telephone receiver back into its cradle. "A disgrace. A *vergogna*, that's what it is."

Her brother Sal had just thrown their mother out of his newly rented flat when Concetta arrived with linens to make up his marriage bed.

" 'Take your sheets and go home,' he told your grandmother," Josie bit out with a scowl. " 'My bride's virtue is no concern of yours.' What kind of way is that to talk to your own mother? No wedding sheets? What will the people say? It's a disgrace."

But Jenny understood. Uncle Sal's Louisa was demure and chaste, a shy young woman he had met at the Italian Protestant church. Sal knew she was virtuous and that was enough for him. He wasn't about to hang out their wedding linens to prove it to anyone.

"Enough already with these old customs!" Jenny told her mother. "Ma, we aren't in Sicily anymore. I'm twenty-four! Louisa isn't going to shame the family, just like my sisters and I aren't going to shame this family. We are good girls. It's time to start acting like Americans. Don't make my sisters go through the same thing I've had to. Enough with taking my brothers on my dates."

From Uncle Sal and Aunt Louisa's wedding on, things began to change. Nino and Josie were not happy about relaxing the choke they had on their daughters, but Jenny insisted on it.

Jenny's best friend was getting married a few months later and had asked Jenny to be her maid of honor. Jenny had paid for her bridesmaid's dress and had already gone for the final fitting when her friend phoned and told her she had just chosen someone else to be her maid of honor.

Jenny held the phone and listened in tears as her best friend rushed on. "It's not me, Jenny. It's my parents. They said any girl who goes out with a boy without a chaperone is a loose girl. They don't want you at the wedding."

Jenny couldn't find words to reply. She was beyond consolation. Her friend's capitulation to her parents wounded Jenny more than her broken engagement had, for the unspoken message of her best friend's phone call was that their friendship was over. Any connection with Jenny would cast a stigma on her friend, who, Jenny learned later, had dutifully allowed her wedding sheets to hang from the living room curtain rod.

My mother told me later that she never got over the pain of her best friend turning on her. They were not children, both were in their twenties, and her friend knew my mother was a respectable girl who had obediently followed all the rules without questioning them. Jenny lost her best friend because she dared to be ahead of her time in the old-fashioned Sicilian community, bucking the old ways her parents, her girlfriend, and her girlfriend's parents clung to, desiring to be free and "American."

. . .

With the Second World War, rationing, recycling, and scrimping came to the home front. Schoolchildren sold war bonds, and women flocked to the workplace in record numbers to take over the jobs of the young men who'd left to fight overseas.

Women's styles changed and sleek became fashionable and patriotic. Jenny's stylish skirts became narrower, like her slacks and dresses, to conserve fabric. Since nylon was needed for parachutes, women's hose were rationed. Except for the most special of occasions, my mother went barelegged, simulating the seam of hose by having my aunt Connie draw a line down the back of her legs with eyebrow pencil.

While she was forgoing nylons for the sake of parachutes, the man who would one day become her husband was in the Air Force, packing parachutes and flying planes. Art, her current boyfriend, took Jenny to the movies but never held her hand. He told her he was keeping her from falling for someone else while he saved her for someone special—his best friend. Art introduced the two of them the next time my father, Ray, came home on leave.

Ray arrived back in Detroit at the height of summer's ragweed season, while Jenny was red-eyed and runny-nosed and sneezing from hay fever. At first Josie insisted that Art keep this prospective suitor away until after the first frost killed the pollen in Detroit, but Jenny was having none of that. She'd heard too much about the handsome pilot to sit on the sidelines while he found someone else. Instead, she followed her mother's advice and week after week told her new suitor she was suffering from a very bad—and very long—cold. Josie was convinced that if he knew her daughter had a chronic condition like hay fever, he'd be fearful of catching the allergy from her, or would find her somehow defective as wife material, and would never come back.

In his own household, Ray was catching hell from *his* Italian mother, who'd warned him from the time he was ten never to bring home a Sicilian girl. Unlike *their* family, who'd emigrated from the mountains near Bologna in the north of Italy, Sicilians were nothing but a bunch of cutthroats and thieves, she said, who slept with guns and knives under their pillows.

Ignoring his mother's protests and insults, he continued to keep company with his Jenny and used the education benefits afforded him by the G.I. Bill to enroll in Michigan State University ninety miles away. Like Nino, he was a romantic at heart. Most weekends, Ray drove to Detroit to visit Jenny. In between, he used his fountain pen to tell his sweetheart how much he missed her.

In 1946, Jenny and Ray were married, and celebrated with a reception at the Book-Cadillac Hotel in downtown Detroit. In their wedding pictures, Ray is beginning to bald while Jenny is petite and radiant, with red lips and dark wavy hair. In their wedding pictures, only Ray's mother scowls.

The newlyweds lived together only on weekends, when Jenny would drive to East Lansing to share the trailer Ray had rented. He still had two more years of college to finish and they'd decided she should keep her good secretarial job in Detroit. Phone calls were too expensive, and so Ray did his homework and then penned love letters to his wife.

Within two years, Jenny was pregnant and quit her job to finally move in with her Ray. They bought a bassinet, she found a temporary job, and he continued to study. He graduated from Michigan State University in June, but they did not move back to Detroit. The baby was due in September, and with only three months to go, they didn't want to have to deal with changing obstetricians—even though his name was Dr. Panic.

.   .   .

I was born on the first of September and by rights should have been baptized Catherine, after my father's mother. But Grandma Tintori said she despised her nickname—Katie—and insisted that no grandchild of hers should have to go through life suffering the same fate.

My parents named me after her anyway. Karen—Greek for Catherine.

Chapter Thirty-two ✥

Detroit, late 1990s

How did she find out she'd had an aunt named Frances? I asked my mother, finding another route to talk about the young woman who so obsessed me. My mother told me that as a little girl she used to eavesdrop on her mother and aunts at night. They would whisper and cry about their sister when they thought their kids were already sleeping.

I couldn't approach my grandmother myself, so I asked my mother to ask her what had really happened, but my mother always told me afterward that Gramma had begun to cry and was too upset to talk about it.

Mama told me still another version of Frances's disappearance—that the frustrated Mafioso husband had gone to his father-in-law and brother-in-law and directed them to "take care" of Frances. That later he'd gone into a rage and put a hit out on them when he learned the boys had killed her when he'd only wanted them to "teach her a lesson."

Aunt Grace's eldest son, my cousin Anthony, told me that when our mothers' cousin, Aunt Aggie's son, had visited from New York, he'd brought along an old picture to show to their uncle Michael, Gramma's baby brother who was born in Detroit.

"Is that my mother?" the nephew asked, pointing to a young girl with an oval face.

Uncle Michael looked at the picture and quietly told his

stunned nephew, "That's the one they never talked about, the one that was killed."

"What happened to the picture?" I asked. "I thought everything of hers was destroyed."

Mama said that Uncle Michael had the picture. I screwed up my courage and phoned him one day to ask about it. "That's the one they *murdered*," he bellowed into the phone, and began to cry. "I don't have the picture. I gave it back."

Chapter Thirty-three ❧

My favorite photo of my parents, Ray and Jenny, on their wedding day.

My parents' wedding pictures have faded to a glossy water-color, the sparkling hues gone from the Kodachrome to leave ephemeral Easter egg pastels washed mainly with yellow. These are not their studio portraits, the formal ones shot by a professional in black-and-white and then painstakingly painted so that Mama's lips, already tinged with the ghost of a smile, are permanently stained a dark blue-red and her eyelashes sweep out long and spidery. These are the oblong, white-bordered, color snapshots my uncles took in front of the fountain on Belle Isle in

1946 and printed up in the photo studio they ran from the basement of the family duplex house.

I was a little girl, plopped on the floor in Gramma Mazzarino's dining room with my sister and our girl cousins, when I first saw them while rummaging through the large lower drawer in her grand carved oak buffet. It was stuffed to the top with layers of loose photos I will never see again, many of which survived a voyage across the Atlantic to drown years later in sewer water gurgling in Aunt Gracie's basement. We girls spent afternoons studying the old pictures, never tired of giggling over younger versions of our relatives or calling Gramma from the kitchen to tell us how we were related to the ones we didn't recognize. We cooed over little Auntie Grace, a Shirley Temple double with her hair hanging in blond corkscrews. We tittered at the stylish bride waving to well-wishers lining a street in Sicily. Gramma's niece, she told us, leaving for her honeymoon with her hat cocked just so, her sleeveless suit cinched with a smart belt, and her right arm raised high to flash us an armpit appallingly black with hair.

In that sea of black-and-white photos, those wedding snapshots surfaced as a spot of color. My favorite looked like a still from a Hollywood extravaganza. My parents stand at the center, mom's white satin peau de soie gown gleaming in the sunlight, its skirt arranged in long gathers and swirled forward to one side while her attendants' huge multicolored bouquets rim the length of scalloped hem. The bridesmaids sit side by side on the grass, weight poised on their right hips, legs stretched daintily away to the left to let only a gemlike tip of dyed-to-match satin pump peek from beneath their gowns. Flanking Daddy, his groomsmen, in cravats and matching cummerbunds, have dropped to one knee with their opposite elbow perched jauntily across the bent leg, which points to the bride and groom. Behind them, a magnificent wedding cake of a fountain cascades down in layers crowned by the ghost of a rainbow arcing from the mist that haloes the uppermost tier.

The outer bowl of the Scott Fountain, reached by steps, was dotted with stone dolphins, lions, and turtles spitting streams of water. Three concentric marble rims surrounded the fountain's centerpiece, a high bowl capped with a basin perched on carved figures. Water jets circling the rim sent spray curving through the air, and a single jet at the fountain's tippy top shot skyward like a geyser.

Belle Isle was one of the most magical places of my childhood, an island park a mile upstream from downtown Detroit, an oasis of greenery and flowers just a short bridge span from the city shoreline. Designed by Frederick Law Olmsted ten years before the famed architect would create the 1893 Chicago World Fair's White City, Belle Isle was home to an aquarium, a forest preserve, a Coast Guard station, the Detroit Yacht Club, and the only marble lighthouse in the world. Each weekend shiny cars plastered with hundreds of white Kleenex carnations snaked along its lanes bringing newlyweds to wait in turn to pose before the fairy-tale fountain. On hot summer Sundays we often rode around Belle Isle after dinner to cool off and stayed past dark, parking the two-tone white and turquoise Chevy to watch the water dance down the fountain's marble tiers to the pulse of changing pastel lights.

The Belle Isle of my parents' day was a triangular-shaped park dotted with cast-iron barbecue pits and wire trash cans rusting alongside sturdy wooden picnic tables. Families came in droves to canoe and hike and picnic beneath oak trees so enormous their roots sank like anchors into the riverbed. At night, couples danced to live big band music in the bandshell, and in a gentler time even brought their sweaty children there to sleep on blankets beneath the stars when the summer city heat made ovens of their bedrooms.

Growing up, I stared out at the water of the Detroit River from Belle Isle, I canoed along the canals, but I never swam there.

The water phobia that runs through my mother's family like an undercurrent surfaced every summer of my childhood in the shrill voices of my aunts and mother and grandmother screaming us constantly back to the shallow end.

"Why do we have to wait an hour to go in the water?" we'd whine after lunch.

"Because you can drown on a full stomach, that's why."

Sitting sweaty and impatient in our bathing suits, we'd glare and wheedle and whine at our ridiculously overprotective matriarchs.

"No we *won't*," we'd moan, back when we were brave enough to edge out to the buoys but still leery of releasing our grip for long on the ropes stretched between them. "Why do you have to be so afraid of the water?"

"Because Aunt Grace nearly drowned when she was little. And look what happened to her back."

Aunt Grace had a curvature along her spine, and I was an adult before I learned she was born with scoliosis. My mother told me her sister's back became crooked because someone at a beach had pushed her backward into the chains that roped off the shallow area from the deep.

It was my first lesson that swimming was a dangerous thing.

I am still a tentative swimmer. A white-knuckled boater. I love the water—but from a distance. Waves lapping against a shoreline, I'm rocked to sleep. A wide expanse of azure glistening toward the horizon, my blood pressure sinks with a sigh. But the mere thought of inching into a pool, a lake, or a river chokes my breath off high in my throat and jump-starts a terror thudding in my chest. I will always remember what it's like to drown. In a heartbeat I am there. . . .

I began to hyperventilate once in Hawaii as I forced myself to let go of the ladder at the back of a boat, the last passenger to plop into the ocean, the only adult snorkler buoyed by an inner tube and still too terrified to dip my masked face into the water. My husband heckled until he'd goaded me into pushing my face into the water, but it took a half hour of gulping down ragged breaths before I could finally convince myself to relax.

My husband doesn't understand why I still have not managed to conquer my fear of water. But he grew up in the fifties in Detroit as a water baby.

Chapter Thirty-four ✤

Me, all of two, with my expectant parents.

Detroit, 1950s

Everyone's house has its own signature fragrance, a distinctive perfume that rushes up to greet you at the door, then fades back into the woodwork even before you've had the chance to hang your coat. It is invisible, elusive, and often undefinable, yet remains a scent so powerful, so personal, that one whiff can trigger a lifetime of memories. Part cooking, cleaning, dust, and sweat, it is an evocative essence that seeped into the walls like a final coat of paint.

My grandparents' house smelled like Italy—redolent with heady aromas of olive oil, garlic, tomato paste, and basil. Inhale deeply enough, and you could catch an underlying scrubbing that was part Murphy's Oil Soap and part Old Dutch Cleanser.

Their yard smelled of roses. The front and one side of the red brick duplex was trellised with roses climbing in reds and pinks. Their perfume circled the house. The backyard was rimmed with a chain-link fence lined with more roses. Interspersed among those multicolored bushes, single roses Grandpa had cut from a bouquet or from someone else's yard hibernated beneath dew-filled mason jars that he'd screwed into the earth. Each jar glistened in his garden for a year, until Grandpa could see the first sturdy shoots of a new bush inside.

The only commercial blooms we ever saw in their house were the ubiquitous foil-covered pots of Christmas poinsettias and white Easter lilies our parents bought on the holidays and crammed around the television set.

After driving his produce truck for a number of years, Grandpa Mazzarino had taken the advice of a relative to establish a permanent location, and he purchased a busy corner lot on Detroit's east side. Nino parked his produce truck on the lot, and for a change the customers came to him. With his profits, he expanded several years later, building a small produce stand there. While my mother was pregnant with me, he decided to pull out his trowel and mortar and go into the restaurant business. Brick by brick, he built his restaurant on that corner with his sons, Dom and Sam, and hired out only the electrical work.

The restaurant smelled of chili and spaghetti sauce and cigarette smoke and burgers frying on the grill. When Grandpa tossed his homemade bread dough into the air and caught it on his fists, stretching the base for a pizza to slide onto the bricks in the oven out back, nothing surpassed that aroma of oregano, garlic-fried mushrooms, tomatoes, pepperoni, and stringy melted cheese.

"The restaurant," we always called it—my grandparents' second home, and one of the most exciting places of their grandchildren's childhoods.

Mr. Nino's was a greasy spoon, a truck stop, and later a high school hangout for "greasers." Huge plate glass windows framed the building's front and sides, and a back wall made entirely of brick bordered the kitchen area. It was narrow, with the refrigerator, sink, worktable, and a pass-through window along the inside wall that bordered the dining area. The commercial-sized gas stove, butcher-block workstation, and the pantry ran opposite, along the outside wall. "Mr. Nino," who stood in the center of his kitchen on platforms made of slatted wood, understood ergonomics. He could turn easily from stove to refrigerator without having to take any steps.

The dining area was divided between tables and the counter, which ran the length of the restaurant, bulging like a horseshoe to face the centered front door. Round blue vinyl seats that swiveled on chrome posts rimmed the counter set with chrome napkin holders, salt and pepper shakers, tall pourable sugar jars, and squat chunky jars filled with Parmesan cheese and hot red peppers.

A double-tiered glass pie case sat at the far end, near the entry to the lavatory and the kitchen. Its bottom shelf was stuffed with packs of chewing gum and candy bars. Opposite stood the soda pop dispenser, right above the ice cream freezer lined with shiny metal sundae dishes.

Square Formica-topped tables filled the perimeter of the room, with blue vinyl and chrome chairs to seat about forty more patrons. A pay phone booth with a hinged door took up one outside corner. A huge jukebox aglow with colored neon lights sat to the left of the front door, and the cigarette machine flanked the door on the right. When the restaurant was empty of customers, "Mrs. Nino"—our grandmother Josie—would hurry from behind the counter to lift the jukebox's huge domed glass cover and click a metal latch inside. Two at a time—"No more, Grandpa will get mad because people who will pay can come in any minute"—we could punch in the numbers and letters to select our favorite tunes, playing all the 45-rpm records we wanted for free. Once a month, after the jukebox man had updated the play list, Gramma would let us help ourselves from the stack of worn black discs piled on the shelf beneath the pie case.

We ate at the restaurant nearly every week, usually burgers or pizza, but we loved best the Cokes Gramma let us make, always pressing our glasses very slightly against the dispenser so that more syrup flowed than soda.

Though the board of health would have viewed it otherwise, Gramma thought it just fine to put us to work waiting on an occasional table, swiping one clean with a dishrag, or washing the dishes in the square aluminum sink opposite the horseshoe bulge. We were, after all, extra pairs of hands sent to her by God. She'd scoop a quarter from the coins left behind as her tip, and with a wink and one finger to her lips so we wouldn't alert Grandpa, she'd slip us an *allonzu*—an allowance.

While I was still in grade school, she gave me one of her engagement rings, the one with the tiny ruby-colored stone Grandpa had given her in July. She gave my sister a delicate flowery one set in aquamarine and my mother the large square garnet. Gramma was generous, but she expected everyone to jump to fulfill her demands. It took years before I understood why my father called her the "benevolent dictator."

When our mother wasn't around, Gramma served us coffee— never more than a quarter cup—laced with sugar and lots of warm milk. We felt like big shots sipping it by the spoonful from the restaurant's stubby ceramic coffee cups. From her lips, we learned how to curse in Sicilian and the gist of a bawdy Sicilian song about a girl asking her mother to find her a husband. She was the only grandma I've ever known who talked earthy to her grandchildren and whose face crinkled with laugher when she told us *"va caca ti"*—to go take a crap—and worse.

. . .

With the help of a hired waitress, my grandparents ran the restaurant from three in the afternoon until they closed at midnight or one. My uncles Dom and Saverio and another waitress opened bright and early, doing prep work and covering the day shift. Except for the Coney Island chili, which they bought in huge cans, they made everything, from spaghetti sauce to french fries, from scratch. Even the hamburger patties were freshly pressed out back and stacked in the fridge between two pieces of waxed paper. The restaurant—like the barbecue grills at Belle Isle—was the men's domain, and Grandpa and my uncles reigned in the kitchen.

A short-order grill and a deep fryer sat below the pass-through counter on the dining side, where the men would fry eggs, onion, hot dogs, and hamburgers while talking with the customers with a cigarette dangling from their lips. Through the window we could watch Grandpa in the kitchen, making the pastas, pizzas, and meat dishes. He hit a small bell each time he slid an order onto the shelf, then ripped the next meal ticket from the spindle, asked my grandmother to tell him the order, and looked out to assess the customer before he began to cook.

"Why you have to give so much food?" Gramma would throw up her hands in distress. "You gonna give away all our profit."

"He was a big man. I looked. A big man needs more to eat."

One night I watched Grandpa chop off the end of his thumb with a chef's knife as he rapidly sliced potatoes into fat sticks for french fries. I winced as he grabbed the end of his thumb from the cutting block and set it back into place with a plastic bandage. He went back to cutting his fries and laughed when I begged him to go to the hospital a mile away for stitches. Ever a grafter, he managed to knit that thumb back together with a Band-Aid.

My most vivid memories of the restaurant are of sitting at a table quizzing Gramma for her citizenship test.

"If I don't get this right, they're not going to let me stay here in America," she told us. "Make sure now that I get it right."

"Who are the state senators?" we would ask, reading from the book of sample questions and answers.

"Joseph McNamara and Filippe Hart," she'd say.

"Who is the president?"

"Abraham Lincoln," she'd crow, intentionally giving us the wrong answer with a twinkle in her eye.

Many times we'd burst into tears, petrified. "No, Gramma, no." We'd feed her the right answer and then ask again.

"Abraham Lincoln!" she'd insist, triumphant, while we sat terrified that she was going to flunk her naturalization test and be sent back to Italy.

We had no idea then that her brother Angelo had met that fate, deported back to Italy as a criminal. And it would be decades before I learned from my mother the story of Rocco's visit to Angelo's widow and children in Palermo years after Angelo had died.

"Tell us stories about our papa's life in America, Zio Rocco," they'd said. "He was a rich businessman there, right?"

Ever the cruelest of the Costa boys, Rocco would never have considered sparing his sister-in-law and her children by leaving them with a white lie.

"Businessman?" Their American uncle had snorted in their faces. "He told you he was a businessman? Hah. Your father? He wasn't nothing but a pimp."

Chapter Thirty-five ✦

Detroit, 2000

Seven years had passed since I learned about Frances, and still
she haunted me. My questions had sparked others in the family to press their own parents for information. When Aunt Aggie's
son decided to confront his mother about the girl in his picture,
she broke down in sobs and told him she was eleven years old
when Frances was murdered, and that she remembered the day
her mother barred Frances from coming into the family home.
Aggie watched as Concetta told her second daughter she was a
whore and had disgraced the family and shoved her away from the
door and onto the porch, while Frances begged to be let back in.

Aunt Aggie told her son that his grandfather Domenic had
married Frances off into a prominent Mafia family when she was
thirteen. That it was her father, Domenic, and eldest brother,
Rocco, who had killed her, cutting off her hands before they
drowned her so she couldn't swim. Aggie said that the Mafioso
loved her sister, and went crazy when he found out his in-laws had
killed her when he'd only wanted her warned and that he'd put a
hit out on Domenic and Rocco in retaliation.

Aggie said that the day their mother sent Frances away was the
last time she saw her sister. Aggie had stared out the window as
her older sister picked up her wooden suitcase and watched until
Frances had disappeared down the street.

Chapter Thirty-six ❧

Gramma Mazzarino and me.

Detroit, 1950s

My mother's baby sister, Grace, was in the eighth grade when Gramma and Grandpa began working second shift at the restaurant, which meant leaving the house before she came home from school. She was their first daughter to be left unchaperoned, their first to graduate from a Catholic high school.

They bought her a white-topped, dark green convertible as a

graduation present, and she rolled the top down and whizzed me off to see *The Wizard of Oz.* Gracie could drive at will at eighteen, but my mother was in her midthirties before she first sat, terrified, behind a steering wheel. And while my sister and I were permitted to take driver training at sixteen, we were not allowed to obtain our driver's licenses until we were eighteen or to drive alone until we were nineteen. In Italian families, sometimes progress travels in reverse.

Aunt Grace married at twenty-one, and she and Uncle Sam asked me to be a flower girl. I was a pudge in a dress of yellow taffeta with an itchy net overlay, and between the wedding breakfast and the evening reception, we posed for formal pictures at the Agdan Studios before the pom-pom-covered entourage headed out to Belle Isle.

Gracie was the last of the Mazzarinos' kids to be married, and hers became the final wedding snapshots our family took in front of that magical island's fountain, misted in spray.

She often referred to herself as Auntie Crazy, which was fitting, for her bawdy sense of humor surpassed her mother's. She asked each of her nieces, sincerely but without success, if she could stand as a bridesmaid at our weddings, and we always stood petrified when it came time to open her "extra" shower present, something that was always off-color and mortifying.

I'm certain my mother had mixed feelings about her younger sisters' high school educations and newfound "American" freedoms, even though she'd been the one to champion them. She was proud of her business-school certificate, she was a bright woman, yet we knew her aborted education left her with feelings of inadequacy. She'd often say, "Your father always said, if I'd gone to college, I could have . . ." and she'd shake her head, her voice would trail away, leaving her "possibilities" unspoken.

Yet no matter how many times we kids told, reassured, or insisted to her that she could ace the GED equivalency exam, she remained adamant and we knew she was afraid to try.

Instead, she shifted her educational dreams onto us. From the time I was in grade school, my parents made sure I knew their game plan for me:

I *was* going to college.

I *wasn't* getting married until I graduated from college.

I *wasn't* moving out of their house until my wedding day.

I bristled at their old-fashioned Italian mentality, but I was powerless to change their plan.

As the eldest, I was also obligated always to set a good example not only for my siblings, but for my younger cousins as well. Because my mother was the eldest, and always worried about what others would think or say about us—and therefore about her—she demanded that my sister and brother and I behave perfectly. Mama and Daddy could pin us with a look, and we'd quiver in dread of the consequences that awaited once we got home.

There wasn't any question that we would attend Catholic school, the same one our father had gone to in the sixth grade after a stint in the public school. Sister Marie Concepta, his sixth-grade teacher, also became mine.

We could have gone to White School, where Daddy had started out, but my parents were convinced that the good Dominican sisters would provide us with a superior education. They committed to sacrifice and scrape together the tuition for the three of us. Time and again they told us that they were paying for our education twice, once with their taxes for public school, and again by scrimping for our parochial school education.

In the evenings, we sat at the kitchen table to do homework, and Mama quizzed us on our spelling words while she ironed. When we brought home As, she praised our hard work and told us that next time we'd bring home A-pluses. When I was still in grade school, she told me: "Raise your hand if you know the answer, Karen Ann. Every time. Never—never, do you hear me?—

keep your hand down and let a boy answer the teacher's question if you know what that answer is."

Yet our parents refused to teach us Italian as we were growing up, saying we could pick it up on our own later. We hadn't picked up much more than the curses and the phrases even the Polish kids in the neighborhood knew. We knew little vocabulary and nothing of grammar. Mama spoke Sicilian, her first language. She'd learned English only when she started school. Though Grandma Tintori was born in Illinois, her parents and husband were born in Emilia Romagna. My father spoke their native dialect to his mother's mother, my *nonnina*, who never learned English. My parents thought like many first-generation American-Italians. They loved their heritage, but they wanted their kids to be American.

Later, my journalism degree required two years of language and I decided it was time to learn Italian. My father insisted otherwise.

"That you can always pick up," he said yet again, as if the vocabulary and grammar had passed to me through my mother's milk. "You need to take something useful, like Russian."

I was already married with two children of my own when I happened to catch Connie Francis on a morning television talk show. In discussing her life, she admitted she had rushed into an early and disastrous marriage because her Italian father had told her there were only two ways she was ever leaving his house—in a white dress or in a coffin. I understood.

Bucking the Italian ways had resulted in unhappiness for her, but—unlike me—at least she'd had the guts to rebel.

Chapter Thirty-seven ❧

Detroit, 1960s

A thick canopy of elm branches twined above our street, over-shadowing the streetlights that spilled soft light onto our sidewalks at night. Wooden shingled houses lined our side of the block, while Saint Augustine's buildings sprawled down three-fourths of the opposite side of our street. Only five houses sat be-tween the convent and the side street, bordered by a huge, fenced playing field, that stretched toward our library outside Ham-tramck. From our dining room window, we looked out onto a va-cant lot pocked by billboards and then across Davison Avenue to the bus stop. We grew up in Detroit at a time when kids could leave the house to play with friends after dinner and then walk home after dark by themselves without their mothers bothering to worry.

Though it was years before we could cross the street each morning for school—with a traffic light, with a safety boy—without a wave of permission from Mama watching us from the dining room window, we did walk almost everywhere. While my grandmother and her sisters had been consigned to the front porch, my sister and I sat out on ours at night with our friends, male and female, our only light that which spilled from the living room window. While my mother and Connie and Grace had to run to the corner store for their mother in pairs, my sister and I were free to roam our neighborhood alone. We hoofed it to the A&P for groceries, to Kowalski's for lunch meat, to the drugstore, the library, the bakery, and to the chicken man to select dinner from a cage and then wait holding our nose in his smelly store while he chopped off its head and feathered it. My sister and I even walked the half hour to Hamtramck to buy presents for our parents for their birthdays and Christmas.

Once Mama had learned to drive and we got a second car, she could clip food coupons from the papers for all the stores and then spend an entire morning driving between the A&P, Chatham, and Food Fair to scoop up every sale. The gas she used was negligible compared with what her coupons saved her. Besides, she had grown up running on foot to several neighborhood stores, each for a specific item.

At twelve, Aunt Grace had been allowed to stay home alone after school. At thirteen, I was riding the bus alone to sewing lessons a half hour away. The malls didn't begin sprouting in the outskirts of Detroit until we were teens, so many Saturdays my sister and I would hop on the Davison bus and transfer at Woodward so we could spend a day shopping at Hudson's and other stores downtown.

While the girls in my class had all been allowed to wear nylons, heels, and makeup in the seventh grade, my mother had dug in her own heels. Though I was mortified by my Mary Janes and anklets, and could not hide my hairy legs and armpits, she insisted that I was not yet old enough to shave. Thirteen, she reasoned, was soon enough for garter belts and seamed stockings. I even had to beg her for my first training bra.

Dating?

"Don't even think about it until you are sixteen."

She'd called me into her bedroom when I was twelve, pulled a booklet on menstruation published by Kotex from her underwear drawer, and told me to read it and come to her if I had questions. I got more sex education from girlfriends and Aunt Gracie's shower presents and the nuns who yelled at the boys to keep their hands out of their pockets during class.

I spent my childhood riddled with guilt over sins I hadn't even committed. I knew French kissing was a sin and that petting would send me to hell if I died before I'd gone to confession. Mama and Gramma Mazzarino warned my sister and me over and over that no one ever bought the cow when they could get the milk for free.

The nuns had plans of their own for me. During my sophomore year, while I was chasing after the Beatles, I was running like hell from the Dominicans pursuing me with their conviction that I had a vocation and would enter their motherhouse in Adrian right after high school.

Junior year, the rug came out from under me. Vatican II brought with it guitar masses, English, and meat on Fridays. The rules changed in the middle of the sixth inning and everything familiar was suddenly gone.

I missed the Latin, I missed the organ, I missed the guilt. I'd spent sixteen good years worrying about burning in hell for eternity over sins that were no longer listed in the no-no column.

I continued on at Saint Augustine—I'd grown up with my classmates since kindergarten, we were like siblings—but I had no interest in going to Sunday Mass. It wasn't Mass anymore in guitar and English, it was more like kumbaya.

The nuns were horrified, and so were my parents.

I began thinking about Catholicism, its roots, and Judaism. Jesus was Jewish, and he died Jewish, didn't he? Judaism hadn't changed, I thought—knowing nothing then about Orthodox, Conservative, or Reform branches. It had held true to its traditions, to Hebrew, to the Bible. I borrowed several books from the library and began to read about Judaism and the early church, discovering that if not for the sticking point of male circumcision, the early church might have kept its Jewish bedrock—and I might quite possibly have been born Jewish instead.

Suddenly my great-uncles' abandonment of Catholicism didn't seem so strange to me.

Besides, hadn't my mother often told me that I'd got the features she'd pined for? Told me how she used to sit in school and listen to her teachers with her thumb pressed into her chin and her index finger pushing up the tip of her nose because it might produce two of the three things she wanted: a dimpled chin, a pug nose, and to be Jewish, because Jesus was.

Chapter Thirty-eight ❧

Detroit, late 1990s

More time passed, yet little additional information about Frances surfaced. I searched the vital records in Detroit and found no evidence that she had ever been married there. No wedding license, no intention to marry is listed in the public records, either before or after my grandparents', for a Francesca Costa.

I checked the 1920 Detroit census and discovered that Frances and Josie were the only siblings who no longer lived in the family home that year.

The ship's records I'd ordered arrived, and Frances was listed on the document. In 1997, with the help of an Italian friend to whom I gave only Frances's name, I secured a copy of her birth certificate from Corleone.

It is my ultimate proof that my grandmother did have a third sister. Frances was no figment of anyone's imagination.

Chapter Thirty-nine ❖

Detroit, 1966

The September of my senior year, Grandpa and Gramma Mazzarino celebrated their fiftieth anniversary by renewing their vows at Holy Family Church. Their original attendants once again witnessed their promises to one another, and one by one, their five children ceremoniously walked down the aisle with their own families to fill the front pews of the ornate Italian church.

Outside of my cousins' baptisms or first communions, it was the first time I'd seen my grandparents attend Mass. Everything they did religiously was home based. A plaster statue of Saint Anthony, my grandfather's patron saint, dominated their dining room sideboard, standing three feet tall, with rosaries draped over his arm and vigil candles twinkling at his feet. Crucifixes, rosaries, holy cards, and various statues filled their home. A glow-in-the-dark plastic Saint Christopher rode protectively on their dashboard. But they never attended Sunday Mass. My mother said they were too tired after working until closing time on Saturday nights, but I worried that my otherwise religious grandparents were headed for hell. I had no inkling that they had grown up with the peasant distrust of clerics who were also overseers, first for the wealthy land barons in Sicily, and then for the wealthy church, which bought up the fields after the reunification of Italy.

Friends and relatives packed the banquet hall for the reception following Mass. My grandparents sat at the head table, flanked by their children and their spouses. We cousins, nearly twenty of us, packed the dance floor. Although they looked every bit of their seventy-five and sixty-five years, Grandpa could still spin Gramma in a spirited tarantella. He was painfully shy about public demonstrations of affection, except to his grandkids, and so, repeatedly, we clanked our silverware against our glasses just to watch him have to kiss her in public. At the end of the party, Gramma winked and told us that the two of them were leaving to spend the night at a hotel. And they did.

She made no bones about liking sex. Ten years later, after Grandpa had had a series of strokes, he could get around only with his walker. When it was time to use the bathroom, Gramma would toddle along at his elbow and squeeze herself between the toilet and the bathtub to unzip my grandfather's pants and help him pee.

"I hold him this way, I squeeze him that way," she moaned to my mother, many times. "And nothing. Not a thing. My sex life is over."

During my senior year in high school, my family left the city of Detroit for the suburbs. While Daddy had taken us on numerous Sunday drives to scout out new model homes, nothing had ever come of it and we were glad. We couldn't imagine leaving our neighborhood or our friends. Then, in February, without warning, our parents told us we were moving to Warren at the end of the month.

Since my father's insurance agency was a half mile from our Detroit house, he promised to drive me in each morning so I could graduate with my friends. Mama would make the drive from Warren in the afternoon to pick us up. The following year, while I rode the bus downtown to classes at Wayne State University, my sister and brother would transfer to public school.

We never did learn why they felt it necessary to keep the new house secret from us through all the months it was under construction. Maybe they worried it would jinx the deal. We learned later that just before the drywall went up, they had decided this new house was an end to their spate of lousy financial luck. They nailed horseshoes tightly wound with shiny red satin ribbons between the studs in the walls of every room in the house.

Only after we had spent our first summer in Warren did they discover that, like drinking glasses in kitchen cupboards, horseshoes must always be positioned with the open end pointing up, never down. Down, they learned, was equivalent to dumping your luck away.

Frantic, they sought the advice of an old Sicilian-born priest. His eyes grew wide and frightened. Agitated, he told them that the only fix was to rush out and buy twice as many horseshoes as they'd hung inside the walls, then to wrap them in shiny red ribbon. He came to the house to bless them loudly with holy water and directed my parents to hang the new horseshoes over every doorway and window to counteract the negative drain of the hidden, unlucky ones.

Similar superstitions survived transplantation to America, especially among Italian Americans with Sicilian roots. My greatgrandmother Concetta wasn't the only one in the family who bargained with heaven—my mother was another expert at it. In 1965 she saved my father's life by swearing off potato chips, the tantamount sacrifice for a petite woman who could polish off a one-pound bag of New Eras while watching a TV show and never gain an ounce. The night of his first heart attack, years before his second heart attack, his subsequent triple bypass surgery, and the third heart attack that killed him, my mother poured her heart out to God and swore she'd never eat another potato chip if He let my father live.

Forty years later, at a family picnic, my sister and I were grazing on appetizers with Mama and our stepfather of nine years. She munched on the nacho chips and salsa, sampled the cheddar corn curls, and sipped her wine.

"I love potato chips," she said, her voice almost wistful.

"So, have some," I said, selecting one that had curled over on itself in the frying.

She glared at me as if I'd just dropped "the F word."

"You know I gave up potato chips when Daddy had his heart attack!"

I was flabbergasted that she was still on the wagon.

"Ma! He's been dead twelve years!"

"But I made a promise to God."

I could feel my eyebrows shoot up. "Ma! But he's *dead!* That contract expired. I think that God will think it's okay for you to eat a potato chip."

She scowled at me, her jaw set and determined as I dunked another chip into the onion dip and popped it into my mouth.

I finally saw her eating potato chips a year later. From the other side of the room, I watched her repeatedly scout out the largest chip in the bowl, then scoop it through the onion dip without a trace of guilt worrying across her brow.

As an adult, I brought up the family's magical thinking—this "God bargaining"—with her and Aunt Connie one afternoon while my sister and I helped them cook dinner.

"That's why my aunt Mary had that lazy eye," my mother insisted, repeating the old wives' tale we'd heard often from her and from her mother before her.

"My poor grandmother, hearing that her husband was killed by lightning like that while she was pregnant with Aunt Mary. The shock, you know? That's what did it."

"Ma!" I catch my sister rolling her eyes, a half smile on her face.

"Ma!" I echo, setting down my paring knife. "That is *not* true. An unborn baby *cannot* get a lazy eye just because its mother hears bad news!"

Scowling, my mother and her sister instantly swiveled from the kitchen counter to confront our heresy. "Oh yes it can!" they blurted out, in a single voice.

Chapter Forty ❧

Newly crowned Miss Columbus Day, 1968.

Warren, 1968

For nearly twenty years, the only fruit Mr. Nino sold was encased in piecrust. Still, he remained a dues-paying member of the Detroit Fruit Vendors Association. I was eighteen and a freshman at Wayne State University when Grandpa brought home the application for the Miss Detroit Fruit Vendors Association contest.

The winner would capture a small scholarship prize and the chance to compete against twelve other Italian clubs' queens for the grand title Miss Columbus Day.

I hadn't burned my bra, but I didn't wear it, either. The same mother who held me back from wearing nylons, heels, and my first training bra pretended not to notice. Flower children were in bloom, women friends at college were living in communes or marrying without discarding their surnames. Feminism was a far cry from my grandmother's and mother's paths, but hadn't Mama planted its germs in me when she ordered me never to pretend I wasn't as bright as a boy?

Yet from the time I was a chubby little girl, I had sat misty-eyed in front of the television listening to Bert Parks sing to the girl in the tiara while I dreamed of one day being a svelte Miss America. Gramma urged me to try for Miss Fruit Vendor—for the scholarship money. Besides, Grandpa had told her there weren't too many fruit vendors with granddaughters in the age range to compete.

I first had to reconcile two parts of me—the budding feminist and the need for outside affirmation that the chubby duckling had become a swan. Then I packed my midriff into a long-line bra, bought a miniskirted cocktail dress in autumn colors, had my hair done up in banana curls, and won the scholarship prize. The Miss Columbus Day competition proved a bit stiffer.

The country was in more turmoil than I was. It was the time of Vietnam, the draft and war protests, of LSD and free love, and of the devastation of the Detroit riots. In a single year, I marched down Woodward Avenue with fellow students chanting "Hell no, we won't go" and stood stunned on the sidewalk in front of the Detroit Institute of Arts staring as National Guard tanks rolled down that same busy north-south artery, now eerily deserted.

That same year I joined the staff of the college newspaper, I noticed that most of my friends happened to be Jewish, and I hauled a guy I was crazy about from the front seat of his car to tell him I really liked him but couldn't keep French-kissing him or I'd go to hell. A tall Protestant, he looked down at me as if I'd lost my sanity. Ignoring the couple we'd gone out with, who were still locking lips in the backseat, he drove me home and never called me again.

Grandpa brought home the Fruit Vendors' contest application again the following year, and Gramma called my cousin Susie, next in age and about to begin college herself.

Susie phoned me and asked if I wanted a second go at it. Overwhelmed by her unselfishness, I went shopping for a new short cocktail dress—and a one-piece bathing suit.

Four years before I would become a charter subscriber to *Ms. Magazine*, I paraded down a runway wearing a white ballgown and then a slimming black bathing suit, and ended the evening with the Miss Columbus Day crown perched on my banana curls.

That October I smiled for so many hours I was sure my face would never stop quivering. Perched high on the backseat of a white Cadillac convertible, I waved to the crowds lined up along Gratiot Avenue and kissed Joey Bishop, who was the grand marshal of Detroit's Columbus Day Parade.

And then it was back to reality as the eldest daughter of the eldest daughter of the eldest daughter. As Gramma Mazzarino had called on my mother to clean the house and then to clean Gramma's friends' homes, she now summoned my mother to her east side Detroit home on Saturdays to pay her bills, or shop at the butcher, or do any of myriad things.

The duty of the first-born daughter similarly passed down the line to me. My mother called on me first to fix her hair, to help her write thank-you notes, to help with chores. There was no liberation of the eldest daughter.

Once, when I was in my bedroom studying for finals, my mother called repeatedly from the kitchen until I snapped the book of Shakespeare's plays shut in frustration and stomped into the kitchen.

"You know I'm studying. *What?!?*"

My mother was at the stove frying breaded steak. Gramma Mazzarino sat watching her from the kitchen table.

Without glancing up from her frying pan, my mother cocked her head toward the lower cupboard to her right.

"Get a can of peas and open it and put it on the stove."

I exploded. I told her she was right there, it was ten inches from her, I was studying, I had a final in the morning, why couldn't she open the stupid can of peas herself?

Gramma Mazzarino had the answer.

"When God gave your mother a daughter, He gave her an extra pair of hands. Now open the peas like your mother told you."

That was the day I decided I wasn't having any daughters. No matter how much I rebelled against this firstborn mantle of scrutiny, example-setting, and duty, I was afraid the mix was too inculcated in me to be suppressed.

My mother, the woman so adamant about her children's education, the same mother who'd resented being loaned out as a young woman to do laundry and housecleaning for her mother's friends, even *she* had succumbed to the "extra pair of hands" syndrome!

What if my genes were so steeped in this pattern that *I'd* end up perpetuating it, no matter how conscious an effort I made not to inflict it on the next generation?

Chapter Forty-one ❧

My mom and me, Miss Detroit Fruit Vendors Association, 1968.

Warren, 1971

Three years and untold hours of reading, questioning, and agonizing later, I sat at our kitchen counter and faced my parents. "This is the hardest thing I've ever had to tell you in my life," I sobbed.

The tears streamed faster as I thought about their sacrifices to send me to Catholic school, about the Jewish tailor, the boss my father credited with giving him a moral upbringing during the five Depression years he spent in his employ. I thought about my long dissatisfaction with Catholicism and about all that I had found in common with my Jewish friends.

"I want to be Jewish." It was out. They were still standing.

I had been dating Larry—the man who would become my husband—for four years, but it never dawned on me that afternoon that my parents might have feared something equally against their strictures—that their sobbing eldest daughter was about to confess she was pregnant.

"If we thought we were losing a daughter," they told me, with more understanding than I as a parent might have possessed, "it would be one thing. But we know we aren't losing you."

They had questions and they had concerns. Converting to Lutheranism or Presbyterianism is one thing, they cautioned, advising me to make certain I knew what I was doing before stepping completely to the other side of the theological fence.

Gramma Mazzarino had some advice of her own. One Saturday while I was alone with her in her house, she told me that I didn't have to convert. She was convinced that Larry was pressuring me. He never had, I replied.

"My younger brothers, when all of them went Protestant when I was young, they convinced my parents to go Protestant, too. And then they came after me and my sisters and told us that we should leave the Catholic Church with them. But I didn't want to leave the Catholic Church and I told them that.

"My one brother, he told me, 'Josie, take this Bible and go kneel down in the corner and pray, and keep praying until you hear God tell you this is the right thing to do.'

"So, like a dummy, what did I do? I took the Bible and went to kneel in the corner like he said. For three days I went to kneel in that corner until I finally thought to myself, 'What's the matter with you? Are you stupid? You're a married woman. Get up! What for are you kneeling in this corner when you know you don't want to be Protestant.'

"So I did—and my brother never asked me to go Protestant again."

I was twenty-three when I began weekly lessons one-on-one with a rabbi, and agonized when he told me we couldn't begin until he had talked with my parents. Bad enough I had told them I wanted to be Jewish. Why did I have to add insult to injury by dragging them off to see the rabbi?

He wanted to tell them that Judaism doesn't proselytize, that I had come to him of my own convictions, and that he had sent me away three times. He wanted their blessing on my studies before we began.

I was converted by a *beth din*—a legal court of three rabbis—at an Orthodox *mikveh* when I was twenty-four. Later that year, Larry and I were married under a *chuppah* by the Conservative rabbi who had taken me on as a student. We spent part of our honeymoon in Italy.

Chapter Forty-two ❧

1984–1985

My father and Grandpa Mazzarino died within two months of each other. My father wasn't yet sixty-four; Grandpa had just turned ninety-three. For years we'd feared that if Grandpa died first, Gramma Mazzarino would throw herself into the grave after him. We were relieved to discover that they had purchased a shelf long enough to house both their coffins high inside a wall crypt.

I learned only after Grandpa died that his father had traveled to the States twice to seek a reconciliation with him. Both times my grandfather refused to meet with him.

For a time, Gramma continued to live on her own in the tiny east side house bordered with Grandpa's rosebushes that they'd moved into long after their former Detroit neighborhood fell into decay. One afternoon soon after he died, Gramma passed my grandfather sitting in his usual place opposite the television. He was dressed and ready to leave the house and told her to hurry up and get her purse because they were late.

Gramma ran the twelve steps to their back bedroom, grabbed her purse, and hurried back to the living room to find his chair empty.

My father came to my mother once, also. Early one morning when she was in deep despair, he scooped her from the bed where he had died, crushed her to his chest, and set her back down again.

The first time I saw him in a dream, we communicated telepathically and he told me he was fine, that there were plenty of green things to eat where he was now. Another time, I told him excitedly about the birth of my brother John's baby daughter and he smiled and said, "I know. I've seen her."

I remember nothing of my Great-Grandma Concetta, although I was two when she died. All I have of her is the four-generation snapshot and other people's memories. She and my great-grandfather moved in with one of their younger sons when they could no longer live alone. Both of them favored only the grandchildren named for them. Domenic was struck by lightning twice more in his adult life—both times he was standing on the same front porch—and survived. Concetta remained crochety until the day she died and took pleasure in whacking her unsuspecting grandchildren on the head with her cane as they passed her by. Aunt Connie told me she was always afraid of her grandmother.

When Gramma Mazzarino could no longer live alone, her three daughters packed up her house and put the Mazzarino mementos in Auntie Grace's basement. Her clothes hung in closets at all three of her daughters' houses, and each Sunday at 10 P.M., one of her sons-in-law would be pulling into another's driveway to drop off Ma. A week at a time, she lived with her daughters, who jumped to her call every time she wanted her sweater adjusted on her shoulders or needed another Kleenex. A week at a time, she ruled their roosts like a queen mother and told her grandchildren, "My life is shit. I'm a gypsy."

Chapter Forty-three ❧

Detroit, 2000

Uncle Louie's son and his wife came for a visit from Florida, and Grace's son Anthony and I asked them if they knew anything about their father's older sister. He'd already heard I'd been inquiring and sat us down to tell us what his father had told him.

Uncle Louie's version was that Frances didn't marry the Mafioso because she couldn't. He was already married. Rather, she had fallen head over heels in love with him and had run off with him to be his gun moll.

Their eldest brothers, Rocco and Pasquale, had followed them for several weeks before they kidnapped and murdered her, trying to make it look like a Mafia hit, to save the family honor.

Chapter Forty-four ❧

A year after Uncle Louie's son and daughter-in-law told me Frances was a gun moll, Uncle Louie's daughter read a letter I had sent to her brother, asking him for more information about Frances from his dad. She called me and told me her father was leery of saying too much for fear that people could get hurt. He wept every time he talked about his sister Frances. She had been his favorite, and as a young boy he had vowed to kill his older brothers to avenge her when he grew up.

She told me that her father said that Aunt Frances was promised to the Mafioso but instead married the young barber, whom she loved. That she ran away with him, and when she returned, Uncle Rocco had stoned her to restore the family honor. That Rocco then went to the Mafia to brag about what he had done but that they despised him for it instead.

Uncle Louie told her how his mother changed completely the night his brother walked in to tell them what he had done, how his father had sobbed and his mother had screamed all night so loudly you could hear her two blocks away.

Chapter Forty-five ❧

Detroit, 1919

There was no end to Concetta's screams that awful night Frances was blotted from the family, nor would there be in the nights that followed.

The following morning, Concetta's eldest sons did not leave the house for work. Instead, Rocco and Pasquale headed for the Romanos' house, swaggering with the proof that they had restored the family honor. Certainly now the Romano clan would look favorably on their unflinching resolve, their cleverness and skill.

For a second Calogero could not comprehend what Frances's brothers were telling him, even though he could see that the wedding band Rocco held out to him was rusty with dried blood. A second later he was unable to contain his revulsion.

"You did what?" he snarled. "Oh my God, what kind of animals would brag about doing such a *vergogna* to their own sister?" Rage reddening his face, Calogero advanced on them. "You are worse than vermin! Get the hell out of my house before I kill you both with my bare hands."

In their zeal to prove themselves worthy of the Mafia, the brothers had crossed a line that even their sister's fiancé would never have condoned.

By midafternoon, Domenic and half the Sicilian community had heard the rumblings. The Romanos had put a hit out on Rocco and Pasquale.

Hollow-faced and haggard, Concetta clutched at her hair and keened. She begged the Virgin Mother to save her sons, but she knew they were already dead. There was nowhere her boys could hide. Blood needed blood. It always worked that way. If they had to wait forever, the Romanos would track them down and slit their throats or shoot them in the head and leave their bodies to the rats in the street.

Domenic was beside himself. He knew that a cousin related to Calogero Romano's mother had died, and that all of the Romanos would be at the Calcaterra funeral home that evening to pay their respects. He was left with no choice. He had to go to Calcaterra's after dinner. No one would stab him in the gut in such a public setting. Unaccompanied, he would walk into the funeral home with his head erect and his heart torn in two to request a meeting with the Romano boss.

Domenic had begged before—for work, for an extra bite of bread when he was a little boy. He had never before begged for anyone's life. Now, the fate of his two eldest sons weighed only on him. What in his role as a *consigliere* could he call upon, what could he draw from that would prepare him to grovel for his sons' lives?

In the end, he could only make his appeal as a father.

"Signore Romano, I beseech you. As one father to another father, have pity on me. I am staggered with grief. I beg you. I have already lost a daughter. Please do not have me lose two sons, too."

He returned home that night a man ten years older, terrified of the price he might be asked to pay for his sons' lives. He could barely speak to Rocco and Pasquale but in the end told them with a nod of his head that he'd won their lives.

Ten-year-old Louie sat at the dining room table working on his math problems. He dug his pencil into the page, carving the sums he figured, when he heard his brothers cheer. They were going to skate free.

He stared at the numbers suddenly swimming on the page and swore with every muscle in his young body that he was going to kill Rocco and Pasquale as soon as he grew up.

. . .

Two years later, when Louie was just twelve, the Romanos came calling for a down payment on the favor of sparing Rocco's and Pasquale's lives. They had some collection work for Louie, paying calls on certain people who hadn't made timely returns of the money they owed. Until the first punch landed, no one would suspect the altar boy was there to beat the shit out of them. Though still a kid, he was all muscle and built like a fireplug.

Louie looked at his father, eyes beseeching Domenic to get him out of this. He was supposed to repay his brothers' debt? He served Mass, he went to school, he played the piano, and he wanted no part of mashing in anyone's face unless it was Rocco's or Pasquale's. Domenic stood stone-faced and told the Romano guy that of course his Louie would take care of it.

"Atta boy," the Romano lieutenant said, slapping Louie on the shoulder and dispatching him on his first errand. "Of course you'll do it. And we know you'll do it right." He bent down, his hand clamping into Louie's shoulder, his mouth close to Louie's ear. "You'll do it right or we're going to have to come and kill your mother. *Capiddu?*"

So Louie saved his mother's life, time and again, and when he went to church to serve Mass, he asked God to forgive him. For Louie understood. He understood that he had no choice.

Chapter Forty-six ❧

Detroit, 2002

Uncle Michael died, and Uncle Louie changed his version of the story for a third time.

Frances had run off with an older, previously married Mafioso and had lived with him for about a month. She was eighteen. They decided to get married. She came back home to tell her parents and make peace with the family.

Their father had gone nuts. "You've disgraced the family. You've blackened my face. I should kill you. I could kill you. I ought to kill you." Words to that effect.

So that same day, after overhearing their father, Rocco and Pasquale took her to Belle Isle, raped her, chopped off her hands, tied her feet to a cement block, and threw her in. Then they came home to brag about what they had done.

Their parents went insane. The Mafioso put a hit out on the brothers, which their father had to talk him out of.

Year after year, version after version, none of the stories coincided. Yet all of them had four things in common: Frances was murdered, two men carried out her execution, they drowned her at Belle Isle, Frances was murdered for some reason of sexual impropriety by men with voracious sexual appetites of their own.

And in nearly every one, Frances was the villain. Oversexed.

Disobedient. Gun moll. Brazen. To make sense of the horror done to her, and to conscience living day in and day out with her killers, the family had ascribed all of the blame to Frances. She'd gotten what she'd deserved.

Chapter Forty-seven ❧

Gramma and Grandpa Mazzarino's real wedding
photo. *Left to right:* Nino, Gramma's sisters Frances
and Mary, Josie.

Detroit, 1995

W hen Gramma Mazzarino died, I was no closer to knowing
the truth of Frances's tragedy than I had been when I first
learned of her existence.

Josie's family mourned her deeply, even though she'd lived

long and well and had finally succumbed to old age at ninety-four. As she lay helpless in a hospital bed in the hospice ward, I hung above her headboard a photograph I'd taken of her and Grandpa Mazzarino shortly before he died. They sat laughing, with kids' pointed birthday hats strapped to their heads and their false teeth hanging halfway outside their mouths, where they'd pushed them with their tongues. I wanted the nurses to know what kind of woman my grandmother had been, was.

At her wake, there were other pictures. The funeral director gave our mothers three huge easels on which to arrange Gramma Mazzarino's life. Over the three nights of visitation, my cousins and I laughed over some, cried over others, and told and retold the stories only we could instantly connect with about our grandparents' lives. We laughed ourselves sick over Gramma's myriad superstitions—how she said to never trust anyone whose eyebrows grew together, to never spit in the air or it would land on your face, which meant both don't brag and don't be snide about someone else or you'll get paybacks.

She always made us take a hat off a table and scolded us when we'd rock backward on the back legs of our chairs; both were portents of bad luck. She'd scream if we washed our hair when we had our periods, certain we'd catch cold, and warned our mothers always to make sure there were no dishes in the sink before they went to bed—"You never know who is going to die, and if the doctor or undertaker came to the house, what would they think?"

Ever the optimist, my Gramma—who is going to *die?*

The morning of the funeral, when my cousin Anthony cornered me, breathless, at the cemetery and asked if I'd seen "the picture," I knew exactly the one he was talking about.

Wedding picture? I told Anthony that the only one I'd ever seen was a posed, tinted portrait my mother had of my grandparents in peasant clothing. They were the only ones in the picture.

"That's not their wedding picture," he said. "It never *was*. Don't you see? It's part of the whole lie."

I could barely contain myself. I had thought Frances's photograph was lost forever. That her brothers had destroyed every trace of her existence.

"Where is it now?"

"My ma had it all this time. She didn't say a word. Just set it out there this morning on the credenza. It's in my dad's trunk."

Tears sprang to my eyes the first time I looked into Frances's face. Uncle Louie was right. She was beautiful.

I locked that photograph in my car that afternoon of Gramma's funeral, and went back inside the social hall to toast my grandmother over lunch.

Chapter Forty-eight ❧

With all the Costas dead now, the whole truth of what really happened to Francesca will never be known, but by 2004 I had come to my own conclusions.

Francesca was in love with the young barber her own age whose name is forever lost to our family. Her father, anxious to move his sons up in the ranks of the Mafia during Prohibition, promised her against her will to a prominent Mafioso twenty years her senior. She followed her heart, eloped with her barber, and paid for it with her life. The barber, certain he was next on the hit list—for in Sicily the brothers always went after the man after they'd killed their errant sister—beat it out of town.

Her mother had eloped before her, her sister Aggie, after. Neither of them had met her fate. She blackened the family's face by spurning the Mafia, ruining her brothers' chances, and that was her sin.

I'd looked at all the stories, from all the angles, and in the context of what I knew about Sicilian morals, the story of my grandmother's engagement, and my own upbringing, I decided on the explanation that made the most sense to me, if one can make sense of this honor killing that happened in America, in my own family.

Frances was dead at age sixteen, for daring to step into her future. Her brothers killed her. Whatever she might have experienced or accomplished was extinguished in an act of family violence that has reverberated through our generations, leaving collateral victims in its wake.

Her brothers got rid of Frances and everything she owned—her clothes, her photos, her wedding dress, her name. They destroyed everything except that single photograph of my grandparents' wedding hidden away by my grandmother for more than eighty years.

But although they obliterated her from the family tree, edited her out of the family lore, told the little ones she'd had to "go away" or had "an accident," they did not succeed in erasing her from her younger siblings' hearts.

Uncle Louie pretty much confirmed my supposition later that same year when he came in from New York to visit my mother, who was dying of pancreatic cancer. His daughter told me that if there were no strangers in the kitchen—referring to my husband and my sister's husband—her father would talk to me about Aunt Frances.

I'd brought with me a copy of my grandparents' wedding picture, and after dinner that evening, I handed it to him. His eyes spilled over and he pulled a handkerchief from his pants pocket.

"She was beautiful, my sister," he finally said.

"My brothers killed her at Belle Isle," he told me, "after she came back to say she was married to the barber. I was just a little kid when it happened. It bothered me for years and years. I had to know how. . . ." His voice trailed off.

"One day when we were both men, I asked my brother Pasquale. I knew he was there that night."

"So it was the two eldest brothers," I said, and he nodded.

"Pasquale said he didn't do anything. He just watched."

"He said Rocco chopped her hands off with a shovel, and tied her legs to cement and threw her in."

We sat in silence for several minutes. Then he kissed her picture and asked me if he could keep it.

I haven't been to Belle Isle since I first learned about Frances more than a dozen years ago. I've thought about walking the shoreline there and tossing a bouquet of flowers into her grave.

She has been with me from the day I first heard her story. Some days, I pretend her brothers didn't really kill her—that they only feigned a murder to keep face with the Mafia.

I imagine that she and her barber ran through the woods on Belle Isle and jumped into a rowboat with some rumrunners who spirited them off to Canada. I dream that they lived their lives, raised their children, safe from the family that would have murdered a daughter of its own.

I daydream about her, though I've stopped wondering if she is out there somewhere—in another state, in Canada—for by now, she would certainly be dead. I keep her only picture on my desk, and in her eyes I still seek the answers to my questions.

Did you get to live happily ever after with your barber, Frances?

Did you have a daughter of your own?

Did you teach her how to swim?

Author's Note ❧

This is a true story, although I wish it was not.
Some families' skeletons rattle behind locked doors, clamoring until someone stumbles upon the key. Ours waited seven decades for me.

This story, like my recent book *Trapped*, began as a genealogical quest. I have a keen interest in my Italian-American forebears and the ways in which their lives intersected with American history. Luckily for me, I come from a family of pack rats. No need to inundate Italian government offices with document requests or scour LDS Family Center microfilms and microfiche for ancestors' birth certificates or marriage licenses. All I had to do was ask my grandmother to let me photocopy ours. I had no idea how many years would ensue before that permission came or what I would discover when it did.

It took more than a decade after that to ferret out this story. I questioned relatives, read scores of books on Italian history, the lives of Sicilian peasants, Italian immigration to the United States, and Detroit at the time my grandparents arrived from Sicily just before Prohibition.

From that extensive research, I have pieced together the story of my great-aunt, a woman lost to history. I wasn't present—or even alive—when numerous events and conversations I write about here took place. I learned of them second- and thirdhand, from family folklore and stories and countless interviews. Pieced together with the history of the places and times, I gave myself permission to imagine my great-aunt's life.

If Virginia Woolf could imagine Judith as a sister for Shakespeare, I could easily imagine here. Imagining the lives of women lost to history, women men have silenced, is just as valid for an Italian-American woman of working class background as it is for a Bloomsbury intellectual.

Next was the issue of identification. There are many in my family who still do not know this story—even now, several generations removed from its key event. Every family member who was alive then is now dead. Still, I have elected to change a number of family names and surnames to preserve the privacy of descendants. Some names in this book, however, are accurate.

There was one other obstacle which I overcame early in this journey to publication—my reticence to air the family's dirty laundry, to break the Italian code of silence, *omerta*. Writing more than a decade ago in *The New York Times Book Review*, *Unto the Sons* author Gay Talese asked where the Italian-American family-story tellers were. He posited that aside from lack of financial security and the dissonance of so solitary an occupation as writing for those born into such a gregarious culture, Italian-American writers were mostly silent for fear of bucking our culture's deeply inbred stricture of *omerta*. His essay liberated me to pursue this story.

Acknowledgments ❧

Frances's story took more than fourteen years to unravel. It could not have been written without the assistance of many. A number of them—friends and family—will remain anonymous to help preserve either their privacy or that of others. (Yes, the legacy lingers. . . .) My gratitude to them for helping restore to Frances her name, for keeping her story at the front of their minds, for helping pose questions, and for encouraging me as I pursued the truth. You know who you are and the depth of my gratitude always.

They believed, as did others—my husband, Lawrence Katz, who has loved this book before it was one; my incredible and talented editor, Nichole Argyres, who worked as hard as I did to tell this story the best possible way; Sally Wofford-Girand, my insightful agent, who championed Frances's story; my late mother, Joanne Tintori, who finally came around, and her sister Grace, the one who started it all. Both of them would both have been so proud to have seen the end of the journey.

I am indebted to my brother, John Tintori, and his wife, Mary Cybulski, to cousins Anthony and Lynn and Claire, to writer friends Jill Gregory, Marianne Willman, Kasey Michaels, Leslie LaFoy, Ruth Ryan Langan, and to my former editor, Rosemary Ahern, for reading bits of early drafts and offering perfect advice over the years as I struggled to decide the best way to tell Frances's story.

Thanks to first cousins—my own and my mother's—for aiding

the investigation; to Italian journalist and friend Walter Bellisi, who procured Frances's birth certificate, proving she existed; Kylah Goodfellow McNeill, assistant editor extraordinaire; Brenda Woodward, my most kind copy editor; Elizabeth Curione, for saving me from a "needling" error; Anna Savvides, senior clerk at the Burton Historical Collection Detroit Public Library, for research assistance; Mary Louise Bergishagen and the librarians at the West Bloomfield Public Library, who facilitated numerous interlibrary loans; Charlotte Hughes for endless photocopies; Carolan Kviklys and Tonya Piscitelli, I love yer guts; gratitude to Jasmine Cresswell, Mary McBride, Jill Churchill, Fayrene Preston, Nora Roberts, Maggie Osborne, Kay Hooper, Marianne Shock, Cheryl Weiss, Mary Knoll, Theresa Vitale, Marge Kasparian and her late grandmother, Theresa Testori, and others who have been sounding boards for years and years; the Italian genealogists whose posts on the listservs of POINT and COI taught me fascinating information daily about our Italian heritage and directed me to many important books about the lives of the peasants of Sicily and the Italian immigrant experience. Thanks to my children, Mitchel and Leslie Katz, and Steven Katz, and the Katz and Tintori families for believing Frances's story would get told.

And most especially to Uncle Sal, for confirming that the story I came to believe was the truth, and to writer Gay Talese, whose 1993 essay in *The New York Times Review of Books* freed me from my fear about telling the family secret.

1. How do Frances's experiences in America lead to her elopement? Would she have done the same thing had the family remained in Italy?

2. Would one of the Costa boys have been punished had they defied the family? Who would have meted out the punishment? Would it have been as harsh as Frances's?

3. How and why are certain parental traits passed down to their children (or not)?

4. Clearly, the Church was important in Italian-American society. Did the clergy just look the other way?

5. What about the law? How does a person just vanish, unaccounted for?

6. Do you think Frances anticipated her fate? Why or why not?

7. How did Frances's family handle the relaying of her story and the incredible weight of emotions that were bundled with it?

8. What does Frances's story say about the value of women in her culture? What cultural values impacted that society's treatment of women?

9. How does Frances's story resonate today? What has changed? What remains the same?

10. Do you think Frances's story will have an impact on the present generation of her family?

www.karentintori.com

For more reading group suggestions, visit
www.readinggroupgold.com

CPSIA information can be obtained at www.ICGtesting.com
Printed in the USA
LVOW12s1136070216

474070LV00001BA/156/P